Th
Easy
Vegetarian
Cookbook

CARDOVA
RIOJA

The Gate Easy Vegetarian Cookbook

Adrian and Michael Daniel
Photographs by Richard Jung

Mitchell Beazley

This book is dedicated to our parents and our grandmothers with our gratitude for the love, wisdom, and incredible food we grew up with.

The Gate Easy Vegetarian Cookbook
Adrian and Michael Daniel

First published in Great Britain in 2007 by Mitchell Beazley, an imprint of Octopus Publishing Group Limited, Endeavour House, 189 Shaftesbury Avenue, London, WC2H 8JY
www.octopusbooks.co.uk

An Hachette UK Company
www.hachette.co.uk

This edition printed in 2012

A CIP catalogue record for this book is available from the British Library.

ISBN: 978 1 84533 760 5

Commissioning Editor **Rebecca Spry**
Art Director **Tim Foster**
Executive Art Editor **Yasia Williams-Leedham**
Senior Editor **Suzanne Arnold**
Editor **Susan Fleming**
Designer **John Round**
Photographer **Richard Jung**
Illustrator **Zara Thomas**
Proofreader **Jamie Ambrose**
Indexer **John Noble**
Production Controller **Jane Rogers**

Set in Zwo

Printed and bound in China

CONTENTS

INTRODUCTION

On Adrian's 18th birthday, a few months after he turned vegetarian, we spent a beautiful day on London's Hampstead Heath with friends. As a birthday treat, they took us to a well-known vegetarian establishment. Eating in restaurants was not part of our upbringing, so it was an experience that we anticipated with great excitement. It was early evening, yet the restaurant was already packed with diners. We didn't recognize anything on the menu and happily abdicated responsibility to our equally famished friends, who ordered a selection of dishes for all of us to share. Upon the arrival of the food, which tasted as insipid as it looked, something happened inside us.

Although The Gate was not to be opened for at least another six years, we still feel that this was its moment of conception. We left that restaurant with one thought: that food, especially in restaurants, should be about pleasure and indulging the senses, rather than just sustenance for the body.

It was from this point that we really began cooking and concocting recipes, drawing on the wonderful food that we had grown up with and attempting to translate this into vegetarian cuisine. In 1987 we opened a catering company in north-west London, where many of the ideas and principles that now underpin The Gate began to evolve. The first and most important was that although vegetarians don't eat meat, neither do they desire a diet of indigestible wholefoods. Vegetarians seemed to be in a process of compensation, having omitted so many "unhealthy" aspects from their diet, and we felt the vegetarian cook should feel liberated to use butter and cream and generally

encourage a sense of indulgence. Other golden rules began to take shape as well. Each vegetable has an optimum way of being prepared, be it roasting, grilling, or pan-frying, and the simple alchemy of how water is taken out of a vegetable will often determine its true flavour. It was also during this period, the final years of our grandmother's life, that we got to spend quality time in the kitchen with her, learning some of the wonderful recipes that she brought from India.

In December 1989, we opened The Gate at Hammersmith with a simple mission statement: "We have coffee, we have food, and we have love", an expression that Michael overheard in a Bohemian café in Tel Aviv.

The menu in the early days was limited but as we developed and grew the menus became increasingly sophisticated and the restaurant more popular. In 1993 we were thrilled to be awarded the *Time Out* Best Vegetarian Meal Award. This was a watershed for us! Our quiet little place had finally grown up. It was no longer the hidden hang-out of trainee doctors from Charing Cross Hospital enjoying late-night lock-ins, and neither was there time to pick up buskers from the subway and invite them to play for dinner and a bottle of wine.

In spite of the commercial realities of running a "proper", busy restaurant, we have tried to preserve something of that spirit through our wonderful customers, many of whom have been eating at The Gate for more than 16 years. We hope that you will enjoy cooking the recipes from this book. They reflect the origins of The Gate and the simple home cooking that was its inspiration.

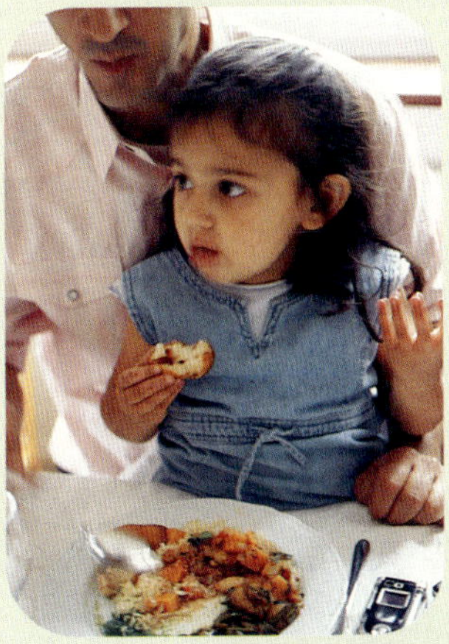

1

Brunch

Brunch has become increasingly popular in recent years. It is an opportunity to indulge in comfort food that we might avoid during the rest of the week, to revive Sunday-morning spirits and ease us into the week ahead. The best brunches last long into the afternoon.

Brunch is not quite breakfast and it's not quite lunch; in our view it's altogether better. It is about unfussy cooking and easy, relaxed dining with friends and the Sunday papers. It's all about flexibility of ingredients – using what's in the store cupboard and even incorporating the leftovers from the night before. Although we have suggested ingredients for our brunch recipes, this is the perfect time to experiment with your own combinations: brunch is a time for inspiration without the pressure of expectation. For example, our *quesadilla* recipe (*see page* 22) will work just as well with a nice lump of English Cheddar and a few pan-fried leeks.

Shakshuka

Shakshuka is a favourite at the Daniel brunch table. Almost every family of Middle Eastern origin, as we are, has its own version of this flavourful scrambled egg dish. This is how we cook ours.

SERVES 4

olive oil 2 tbsp

green chillies 2, finely chopped

red onion 1 small, chopped

tomatoes 500g (1lb 2oz), chopped

salt 1 tsp

eggs 6 medium, beaten

TO SERVE

coriander leaves handful, finely chopped

pitta breads, warmed 4

1 Heat the olive oil in a pan, and add the chilli, quickly followed by the chopped onion and tomatoes. Add the salt and cook for 5–6 minutes until the tomatoes have broken down and the mixture is beginning to thicken.

2 Add the eggs and scramble into the tomato mix for 2–3 minutes. Stir constantly to ensure that the eggs do not burn.

3 Garnish with fresh coriander, and serve immediately with warm pitta bread.

Potato Mamoosa

This simple and quick-to-prepare dish – a spicy scrambled egg with tomatoes and potato – is another one of our favourites, almost the perfect brunch. We love to eat *mamoosa* with warm pitta bread and Apple and Coriander Chutney (*see page* 169), or any other chilli sauce we may have.

1 Heat the olive oil in a lidded frying pan, then add the chilli and turmeric, followed quickly by the chopped onion. Cook the onion on a medium heat for 3–4 minutes until translucent.

2 Add the diced potato and stir well for 3–4 minutes. Cover the pan, reduce the heat to low, and continue to cook for a further 10 minutes.

3 Add the chopped tomatoes, cover, and cook for another 10 minutes.

4 Add the eggs, and scramble gently into the potato mix, cooking for about 3–4 minutes.

5 Season with salt and garnish with coriander. Serve immediately.

SERVES 4

olive oil 2 tbsp

green chillies 2, finely chopped

turmeric 1 tsp

red onion 1, chopped

potatoes 500g (1lb 2oz), cut into 1cm (½in) dice

tomatoes 2 medium, finely chopped

eggs 4 medium, beaten

coriander leaves handful, chopped

salt

Eggs Florentine

We used to cook this dish often at The Gate, when we were open for weekend brunch. It is quick to prepare and makes a lovely, comforting breakfast. We love the flavour of tarragon in a hollandaise, but if unavailable replace with chives.

1 Cook the spinach with the butter in a pan until all the excess water has evaporated.

2 While you are cooking the spinach, bring 1 litre ($1\frac{3}{4}$ pints) water to the boil with the vinegar. Poach the eggs in this for about 1–2 minutes or until the whites have solidified. Remove the eggs from the water with a slotted spoon and place on a warm plate.

3 To finish, toast the halved brioche rolls on both sides. Divide the spinach between the cut sides of the rolls, and place an egg on top of the spinach. Finally, pour over the hollandaise. Serve immediately.

SERVES 4

fresh spinach 200g (7oz), washed well

butter 30g ($1\frac{1}{4}$oz)

brioche rolls 2, halved horizontally

hollandaise sauce 1 recipe quantity (*see opposite*)

POACHED EGGS

white wine vinegar 1 tbsp
eggs 4 medium

Asparagus and Hollandaise

This classic combination makes a perfect light lunch or brunch dish. We sometimes grill the asparagus rather than blanching it. If you wish to turn this into a more substantial dish, you can add a few slices of polenta (*see page* 65) or roasted potatoes with a few mixed leaves.

SERVES 4

asparagus stalks 400g (14oz) medium

salt

HOLLANDAISE SAUCE

butter 225g (8oz)

white wine vinegar 5 tbsp

egg yolks 2 medium

Dijon mustard 1 tbsp

tarragon 3 sprigs

1 To start the hollandaise, gently melt the butter in a small pan. Tilt the pan and pour out the clear butter liquid (clarified butter) into a bowl, separating it from the milk solids at the bottom. These can be discarded. You will need 200g (7oz) clarified butter for the hollandaise.

2 Boil the vinegar until it has reduced to half its original volume.

3 Place the egg yolks, reduced vinegar, and mustard into a food processor and blend for about 10 seconds. Once you have achieved a smooth emulsion, slowly drizzle the warm butter into the blender, still blending. Finally, add the tarragon and blend briefly so that you have a yellow sauce speckled with green. (The hollandaise can be stored for up to an hour in a warm place.)

4 To prepare the asparagus, break off and discard the fibrous ends. Blanch the stalks for 2–3 minutes in salted boiling water. Drain well.

5 Place the stalks on plates and pour the hollandaise over them.

Frittata

We often cook this mega omelette for breakfast the morning after a barbecue, when there are lots of grilled vegetables left over. Use a heavy pan and keep the onions at its base, because this will help prevent the *frittata* from sticking and will ensure a perfect result.

1 Preheat the oven to 200°C/400°F/gas mark 6. Put the mushrooms on a baking tray. Drizzle half the olive oil over them, then season with salt and pepper. Bake in the preheated oven for 15 minutes, ensuring that all the excess moisture has evaporated.

2 Meanwhile, melt the butter and the remaining olive oil together in a heavy ovenproof skillet, and pan-fry the onion for 6–7 minutes until well softened.

3 Meanwhile, blanch the asparagus and broccoli for 1 minute in boiling water, then refresh in cold water and drain well. Beat the eggs, cream, and Parmesan together.

4 Ensuring that the onions are evenly spread over the base of the skillet, place all the cooked vegetables and the torn basil leaves in the pan. Pour the egg mixture over them and bake for 40–50 minutes.

5 To check that the *frittata* is set, insert a knife: there should be no liquid oozing out. When the *frittata* is cooked, allow to rest for 10 minutes before inverting onto a flat dish. Give the base of the pan a few taps before lifting it up and away.

6 To serve, cut the *frittata* into wedges.

SERVES 6

olive oil 2 tbsp

Portobello mushrooms 150g (5½oz), trimmed

salt and black pepper

butter 25g (1oz)

red onion 1 medium, cut into thin crescents

asparagus stalks 6, trimmed

small broccoli florets 100g (3½oz)

eggs 5 large

double cream 100ml (3½fl oz)

Parmesan 75g (2¾oz), freshly grated

basil leaves handful, torn

Grilled Haloumi

Haloumi cheese, with its incredible texture, makes an excellent base for a very satisfying brunch. Using the marinade given here, the cheese can be skewered on sticks for a barbecue, or simply sliced and pan-fried, and served with salad leaves or our Butter Bean, Pickled Lemon, and Mint Salad (*see page* 127).

1 Cut the haloumi into large 2cm (¾in) cubes, and place on a clean tea-towel to absorb excess water for 10 minutes.

2 While the haloumi is drying, place all the other ingredients in a food processor and blend to a paste. Coat the haloumi cubes well with this marinade.

3 Lightly grease a ridged cast-iron grill pan or a non-stick frying pan. Cook the cubes, turning them, for about 1–2 minutes on each side.

SERVES 4

haloumi cheese 400g (14oz)

red onion 1 small, roughly chopped

red chilli 1, roughly chopped

mint, few sprigs

paprika 1 tsp

ground coriander 1 tsp

lemon juice of 1

olive oil 1 tbsp

Prestige

Wild Mushroom Kibbeh

There is something beautiful about discarding nothing and having no waste in the kitchen. These lovely little kebabs look rustic and taste great using rosemary stems as a skewer. This is an ideal dish for a summer barbecue, but it cooks just as well under a grill to serve for brunch.

SERVES 4

rosemary stems 4, approx. 10–15cm (4–6in) long

shiitake, oyster, and chestnut mushrooms 200g (7oz) of each

olive oil 2 tbsp

mixed salad leaves 200g (7oz), to serve

lemon juice of 1

1 Remove the rosemary leaves from the stems, saving the leaves for another dish.

2 Skewer the rosemary stems through the centre of the mushrooms, dividing the types evenly. Brush the mushrooms with half the olive oil.

3 Grill on the barbecue, or under a well-preheated grill, for 5–6 minutes, turning occasionally.

4 Dress the salad leaves with the remaining olive oil and the lemon juice, and serve the kebabs immediately on a bed of salad leaves.

Corn Bread

This can be made in a tray to serve as a breakfast bread, or as muffins. It is a lovely brunch dish, and the muffins are a good complement to casseroles and soups. The bread is best eaten fresh because it dries out quickly.

1 Preheat the oven to 190°C/375°F/gas mark 5. Line a 30 x 20 x 4cm (12 x 8 x 1½in) baking tray with greaseproof paper. Or have ready 12 muffin tins, about 4cm (1½in) deep.

2 Mix the cornmeal, flour, baking powder, sugar, and salt together. In a separate bowl, beat the eggs and milk together.

3 Mix the sweetcorn into the egg mixture and quickly whisk in the flour mixture. Pour into the prepared baking tray.

4 If in a tray, bake for 25 minutes; bake muffins for 15–20 minutes. To check that the bread is cooked, insert a knife and ensure it comes out clean.

SERVES 6

fine cornmeal 200g (7oz)

plain flour 175g (6oz)

baking powder 2 tbsp

caster sugar 1 tbsp

salt pinch

eggs 2 medium

milk 300ml (10fl oz)

sweetcorn 1 ear, kernels removed

Wild Mushroom Bruschetta

This is one of our favourite breakfast dishes when we are up in Scotland on our mushroom-picking trips. There is nothing quite like it when made with freshly picked chanterelles, but it is just as good using oyster or chestnut mushrooms.

SERVES 4

olive oil 3 tbsp

garlic clove 1, crushed

rosemary and thyme 1 sprig of each, chopped

shallot 1, finely chopped

wild mushrooms 500g (1lb 2oz), cleaned and chopped

white wine dash

ciabatta loaf 1

salt and black pepper

rocket leaves 250g (9oz)

cherry tomatoes 225g (8oz), halved

Parmesan 35g (1¼oz), freshly shaved

1 Heat 1 tbsp of the olive oil gently in a large frying pan, and add the garlic, rosemary, and thyme. Infuse together for 30 seconds before adding the shallot and mushrooms. When the mushrooms begin to sweat and exude water, add the dash of white wine. Continue to cook until all the liquid has evaporated from the pan and the mushrooms have a light, oily sheen: about 6–8 minutes.

2 While the mushrooms are cooking, cut the ciabatta into quarters. Brush the cut sides lightly with olive oil and season with salt and pepper. Lightly toast or grill for 1–2 minutes on the cut sides.

3 Dress the rocket with the remaining olive oil and toss with the halved tomatoes and Parmesan shavings.

4 Place a handful of rocket leaves on top of each piece of bread, then sprinkle on your warm mushrooms. Serve.

Quesadillas

Tortillas are tasty and versatile, both at The Gate and at home. A *quesadilla* is basically Mexican cheese on toast, and it's gorgeous. *Quesadillas* can be made into a more substantial meal by serving corn salsa (*see page* 167) and a guacamole with them.

1 Preheat the oven to 220°C/425°F/gas mark 7.

2 For the filling, pan-fry the mushrooms in the olive oil for 5–6 minutes. Blanch the asparagus in boiling water for 2 minutes, and then refresh in cold water.

3 Brush one side of each of four tortillas with olive oil, and place oiled-side down on a baking tray. Divide the cheese among these tortillas, then sprinkle with chopped onion, chilli, the mushrooms, asparagus, and coriander as if making a pizza. Cover each with another tortilla and press together firmly.

4 Bake for 7–8 minutes. Serve hot.

SERVES 4

flour tortillas 8 medium

olive oil 1 tbsp

FILLING

oyster mushrooms 350g (12oz)

olive oil 1 tbsp

asparagus stalks 400g (14oz) medium, trimmed

Gruyère cheese 400g (14oz), grated

red onion 1, cut into fine crescents

red chilli 1, finely chopped

coriander leaves handful, chopped

Bloody Mary Gazpacho

This is the basic Gate gazpacho recipe. It can be prepared up to 12 hours in advance and works equally well with or without the vodka. When preparing this dish at home for brunch, the vodka is an addition that has become more frequent in recent years as we have developed a taste for Bloody Mary. At The Gate we usually freeze a few ice cubes of the gazpacho to garnish gazpacho soup.

SERVES 4

tomatoes 1kg (2¼lb), skinned, deseeded, and chopped

red peppers 2, deseeded and chopped

green pepper 1, deseeded and chopped

celery stalks 3, peeled and chopped

cucumber 1, peeled and chopped

garlic cloves 2, crushed

olive oil 4 tbsp

basil leaves, handful, torn

salt 2 tsp

ciabatta bread 55g (2oz), crust discarded, bread cut into small pieces

vodka, splash

1 Place all the ingredients in a bowl, cover, and marinate in the fridge for a minimum of 2 hours.

2 Blend in a food processor until smooth.

3 Serve cold.

Celeriac Rösti

This simple twist on the classic potato *rösti* makes a perfect companion to many breakfast ingredients, such as pan-fried mushrooms and a poached egg. It can also be made into the centrepiece of any "comfort" meal. We particularly enjoy *rösti* served with roasted vegetables and a cream sauce.

1 Combine the grated ingredients in a bowl, then sprinkle with the salt. Allow to sit for 20 minutes so that the salt draws the water out of the vegetables.

2 Place the mix in a colander and squeeze out any excess water.

3 Put a sixth of the mixture into a 10cm (4in) hollow ring, and pat down well into a burger-like shape, about 2cm (¾in) thick. Remove the ring, and lightly dust the *rösti* with flour. Do the same with the rest of the mixture to make six *röstis*.

4 Heat some oil in a frying pan or wok, and shallow-fry the *röstis* on a medium heat until golden brown: about 4–5 minutes on each side. Drain well on kitchen paper, and serve hot.

SERVES 6

celeriac head 1 small, grated

onion 1 large, grated

potato 1 large, grated

salt 1 tsp

plain flour, for dusting

vegetable oil, for shallow-frying

2

Pasta and Rice

When we were growing up, rice was very much part of our staple diet, given its predominance in the Indo-Iraqi culinary heritage. However, our early exposure to pasta came from the bog-standard two-sauce Italian restaurant, so it wasn't until we started cooking – and exploring Italian cuisine – that we began to appreciate the subtleties and regional variations that real pasta dishes can offer. This chapter gives some of our favourite pasta and rice dishes, and tips for cooking them.

When cooking basmati rice, soak it for a few hours before cooking because this will result in a lighter, fluffier rice. When boiling pasta, season the water well with salt, and keep a little of the starchy cooking water to add to the sauce if it becomes too thick. Another good tip is to cut the vegetables a similar size to the pasta that you are cooking. This will allow the pasta and vegetables to cook evenly together, and gives the dish a visually pleasing structure. It also makes it easier to eat.

Tagliatelle with Spinach, Mushrooms, and Dolcelatte Cream

This is one of our favourite creamy pastas, the Portobello mushrooms giving the cream a delicate beige colour. As with most of the pasta recipes in this book, once the vegetables have been prepared, the sauce should take no longer to cook than the time it takes to boil the pasta.

SERVES 4

tagliatelle 500g (1lb 2oz)

salt and black pepper

olive oil 1 tbsp

red onion 1 small, finely diced

garlic clove 1, crushed

Portobello mushrooms 300g (10½oz), cut into 2mm ($^1/_{16}$in) slices

white wine, splash

baby spinach leaves 75g (2¾oz)

dolcelatte cheese 70g (2½oz)

double cream 125ml (4fl oz)

1 Put the pasta in a large saucepan of boiling salted water, and cook for the specified time, usually about 10 minutes. Drain well.

2 Meanwhile, heat a pan with the olive oil, add the onion and garlic, and cook for 2–3 minutes until the onion begins to soften. Add the mushrooms and continue to cook until softened: about 4–5 minutes. Add the white wine and continue to cook until the wine and the water from the mushrooms have completely reduced.

3 Add the spinach to the mushroom and onion, and allow it to wilt in the hot pan before adding the hot, drained tagliatelle. Toss in the pan and mix well with the vegetables before crumbling in the dolcelatte.

4 Pour the cream over the pasta and cook for a further minute before serving.

Spaghetti with Chilli and Rocket

This is a real lunchtime favourite of the chefs at The Gate, probably because it is so simple and fulfils the chilli craving...

1 Put the pasta in a large saucepan of boiling salted water, and cook for the specified time, usually about 8 minutes. Drain well.

2 Meanwhile, in a large saucepan heat the oil and infuse with the chilli, garlic, and thyme for a few minutes. Add the shallot and continue to cook for 2–3 minutes. Keep stirring to prevent the chilli and garlic from burning.

3 Toss the hot, drained spaghetti into the garlic and chilli. Add the rocket leaves and mix well before serving.

SERVES 4

spaghetti 500g (1lb 2oz)

salt

olive oil 2 tbsp

large red chillies 2, finely chopped

garlic cloves 2, crushed

thyme leaves pinch, chopped

shallots 2, finely diced

rocket leaves 200g (7oz)

Rigatoni with Leeks, Walnuts, and Goat's Cheese

This lovely pasta, which we first ate when we were in Italy for the wedding of one of our chefs, makes an excellent light dish for summer.

1 Put the pasta in a large saucepan of boiling salted water and cook for the specified time, usually about 10 minutes. Drain well.

2 In a large saucepan, melt the butter, add the garlic and leek, and sauté for 3–4 minutes. Add the white wine and continue to cook until most of the wine has reduced.

3 Add the hot, drained pasta, mixing well with the leek, and crumble in the goat's cheese. Finally, add the parsley and walnuts, and serve immediately.

SERVES 4

rigatoni 500g (1lb 2oz)

salt

butter 55g (2oz)

garlic clove 1, crushed

leeks 2 large, roughly chopped

white wine splash

goat's cheese 75g ($2\frac{3}{4}$oz)

parsley leaves handful, roughly chopped

shelled walnuts 35g ($1\frac{1}{4}$oz), chopped into large pieces

Rigatoni with Arrabbiata

The name of this chilli-hot pasta literally means "angry", so it is no surprise that it was the first pasta sauce Adrian fell in love with. The intense chilli and garlic is a real home from home, and it is the only pasta sauce in this book that takes longer to cook than the 10 minutes it takes to boil the pasta.

1 Chop the tomatoes into smallish pieces, sprinkle 1 tsp of the salt over, and drizzle with a little of the olive oil.

2 Heat a pan with 1 tbsp olive oil, and fry the garlic, chilli, and onion together for 2–3 minutes, stirring occasionally to prevent the garlic burning. Add the tomato and remaining olive oil and simmer for 35–40 minutes until you have a rich tomato and chilli sauce.

3 About 10 minutes before the sauce will be ready, put the pasta in a large saucepan of boiling salted water, and cook for the specified time, usually about 10 minutes. Drain well.

4 Add the basil leaves and rigatoni to the sauce, tossing together in the pan for 2–3 minutes until the pasta is well coated.

SERVES 4

tomatoes 400g (14oz), blanched and skinned

salt 1 tsp

olive oil 100ml (3½fl oz)

garlic cloves 2, thinly sliced

red chillies 2, finely diced

red onion 1, finely diced

rigatoni 500g (1lb 2oz)

basil handful of leaves

Penne with Oyster Mushrooms and Sun-dried Tomatoes

This is what we call "stir-fry pasta", in the sense that it is quick to make and best cooked in a wok, where the pan-fried vegetables and herbs bring the whole dish to life.

SERVES 4

penne 500g (1lb 2oz)

salt

olive oil 2 tbsp

garlic cloves 2, crushed

red onion 1, thinly sliced

oyster mushrooms 300g (10½oz), torn

sun-dried tomatoes 70g (2½oz), thinly sliced

French beans 100g (3½oz), blanched

pine nuts 55g (2oz)

basil leaves handful, torn

1 Put the pasta in a large saucepan of boiling salted water and cook for the specified time, usually about 10 minutes. Drain well.

2 In a wok or large pan, heat the oil and allow the garlic to infuse for 30 seconds. Add the onion and oyster mushrooms, and cook on a medium heat for 5–6 minutes, tossing occasionally to prevent burning. Add the sun-dried tomatoes and French beans, and mix well with the mushrooms.

3 Add the hot, drained pasta, pine nuts, and torn basil leaves, and cook gently for a further 2–3 minutes before serving.

Warm Penne and Goat's Cheese Salad

This is a light summer pasta, which is always popular on The Gate's menu. It is a useful way to utilize cooked pasta that may have been sitting in the fridge: simply heat it up by popping it in boiling water for 30 seconds.

1 Put the pasta in a large saucepan of boiling salted water, and cook for the specified time, usually about 10 minutes. Drain well.

2 Marinate the sliced onion, sugar, and vinegar together for 10 minutes.

3 To make the basil oil, blend together the basil, lemon juice, and olive oil.

4 Put the hot, drained penne in a large bowl and dress with the basil oil. Add the onions and their marinade, and the goat's cheese and chickpeas, and mix well together.

5 Finally, toss in the rocket leaves before serving.

SERVES 4

penne 500g (1lb 2oz)

salt

red onions 2, thinly sliced

caster sugar 1 tbsp

balsamic vinegar 2 tbsp

goat's cheese 175g (6oz), crumbled

chickpeas 75g (2¾oz), cooked

rocket leaves 200g (7oz)

BASIL OIL

basil 1 bunch leaves

lemons juice of 2

olive oil 4 tbsp

Arancini

There is something in our cultural make-up that compels us to put stuffings in our food, and this technique occurs throughout our cooking. There is no exception in our approach to Italian food. These delicious, stuffed rice fritters make a lovely starter or canapé served with pesto (*see page* 154) or aïoli.

SERVES 4

olive oil 1 tbsp

shallots 55g (2oz), finely chopped

garlic clove 1, crushed

thyme leaves 1 tsp, chopped

arborio rice 400g (14oz)

vegetable stock 1 litre (1¾ pints), (*see page* 189), boiling

cherry tomatoes 225g (8oz)

dolcelatte cheese 55g (2oz)

Parmesan 75g (2¾oz), freshly grated

vegetable oil 1 litre (1¾ pints), for frying

1 In a large, shallow pan, heat the olive oil, add the shallot, garlic, and thyme, and cook for 2 minutes.

2 Add the rice to the pan with a large ladleful of stock and stir in well. Continue stirring, and, as the stock is absorbed by the rice, add another ladleful of stock. Continue this process for about 15 minutes or until the rice is just cooked. Remove from the heat and allow to cool on a large tray.

3 While the rice is cooling, cut the cherry tomatoes in half and with a teaspoon or Parisienne scoop (melon baller), gently scoop out the flesh of the tomatoes to leave small "shells". Stuff these with the dolcelatte.

4 Mix the Parmesan into the cooled rice. Take 1 tbsp of rice mix in the palm of your hand and pat flat. Place a stuffed tomato half on top of the rice and gently encase the tomato with the rice and mould into a ball. Repeat this process using all the tomatoes, then chill the rice balls for 15 minutes.

5 Heat the oil in a heavy-based pan until almost smoking. Deep-fry the rice balls until golden brown, turning: about 3–5 minutes.

Mahasha

However *passé* stuffed vegetables are in the world of vegetarian food, this traditional Indo-Iraqi recipe of slow-cooked vegetables is a real favourite in our home on Friday nights, when the family sits together for the Sabbath meal.

1 To prepare the peppers and tomatoes, slice about 1cm (½in) off the top. Do not discard the caps. Deseed the peppers and tomatoes, taking care not to break the skin. Save the tomato pulp for the filling. Blanch the spinach leaves in boiling water for 30 seconds.

2 To make the filling, drain the soaked rice and mix together with the grated carrot and onion, the coriander, lemon juice, cardamom, and turmeric. Season with salt and pepper, and mix in the pulp from the tomatoes.

3 Three-quarters fill the peppers and tomatoes with some of the rice mix, and cover with the caps. Lay the spinach leaves flat. Place 1 tbsp of the rice mix on each leaf and fold over on all sides.

4 Take a medium-sized saucepan and brush the inside with olive oil. Put the stuffed vegetables in snugly, so there is no movement. Cover tightly with the lid and cook on the lowest possible heat for about 2 hours.

SERVES 4–6

red peppers 3

tomatoes 3 large

spinach leaves 4 large

basmati rice 450g (1lb), soaked in water for 1 hour

carrot 1, grated

Spanish onion 1, grated

coriander 1 bunch, chopped

lemons juice of 2

cardamom pods 3, crushed

turmeric 1 tsp

salt and black pepper

olive oil 1 tbsp

Khichri

Khichri is a simple and nutritious rice and lentil pilaff, and it is typically eaten with a salad or a good chilli sauce. *Khichri* is best eaten when freshly cooked.

1 Drain the rice. Wash the lentils and drain.

2 In a medium-sized pan, heat the oil, add the turmeric, and almost immediately add the rice and lentils. Cook in the pan for 2–3 minutes, stirring well.

3 Add 700ml ($1\frac{1}{4}$ pints) water and the salt, and bring to the boil before turning down the heat. Cover tightly with the lid and simmer on a low heat for 15–20 minutes (the lid should not be removed until the rice is cooked).

4 Fluff up before serving.

SERVES 4

basmati rice 350g (12oz), soaked in water for 1 hour

red lentils 150g ($5\frac{1}{2}$oz)

vegetable oil 2 tbsp

turmeric 1 tsp

salt 1 tsp

Pilau Musteen

In Indian cuisine *ha ka ka* is a term for the caramelized food at the bottom of the pan, which is much sought after but is usually the domain of the cook. This recipe was introduced to us by a good friend who grew up in Afghanistan. It is a traditional festive rice dish, usually served on special occasions. We particularly love the scent of the rose petals and the flavour of the potato and rice *ha ka ka* at the bottom of the pan.

SERVES 4

basmati rice 500g (1lb 2oz), soaked in water for 2 hours

salt

vegetable oil 2 tbsp

potato 1 large, cut into 1cm (½in) cubes

ground cumin and cinnamon 1 tbsp of each

cardamom cloves seeds of 5, crushed

dried rose petals handful

dried apricots 40g (1½oz), chopped

chopped prunes, raisins, and flaked almonds 35g (1¼oz) of each

1 Drain the rice, then boil in salted water for about 15 minutes. Drain well.

2 In a large saucepan, heat half the oil and fry the potato for 4–5 minutes.

3 Remove the pan from the heat and drizzle the base and sides of the pan with the remaining oil. Place half the cooked rice on top of the potato. Sprinkle the cumin, cinnamon, cardamom, and rose petals over the rice. Cover with the remaining rice and sprinkle over the apricots, prunes, raisins, and almonds.

4 Cover the pan with a lid, and place over a gentle heat for 30–35 minutes. Do not remove the lid, do not stir, do not touch...

5 Serve from the pan, trying to get a bit of everything on each plate, including the *ha ka ka*.

Butternut Squash Risotto

In truth, it took us a while to appreciate risotto, having come from such a strong tradition of rice cooking where the emphasis is always on individual fluffy grains. However, risotto has a culture and philosophy of its own, and the pleasure of one-pot cooking should never be underestimated.

1 In a large, shallow pan, heat the olive oil, add the thyme, garlic, and shallot, and sauté for 2–3 minutes. Add the butternut squash and continue to cook for a further 4–5 minutes. Add the rice and stir to coat with the vegetables and oil.

2 Now slowly put a ladleful of the hot stock into the rice every 2–3 minutes, allowing the rice to absorb the stock before adding the next ladleful. This will take about 18–20 minutes altogether. Stir often.

3 When the rice is cooked, remove from the heat and add the butter and dolcelatte. When this has melted, add another ladleful of stock to loosen the risotto.

SERVES 4

olive oil 1 tbsp

thyme leaves 1 tsp chopped

garlic clove 1, crushed

banana shallots 2, finely chopped

butternut squash 500g (1lb 2oz), peeled and seeded, the flesh cut into 1cm (½in) cubes

arborio rice 400g (14oz)

vegetable stock 1.2 litres (2 pints), (*see page* 189), boiling

butter 55g (2oz)

dolcelatte cheese 55g (2oz)

Rice Stir-fry

This quick and delicious recipe works best with jasmine rice, and is a useful way to utilize any leftover rice.

1 Boil the rice in a large pot with plenty of water for 15 minutes. When it is cooked, rinse in cold water and drain.

2 In a wok, heat the sesame oil and immediately add the ginger, garlic, and chilli. Fry for 2–3 minutes before adding the pepper, mushrooms, and corn. Stir-fry the vegetables for 5–6 minutes until they begin to sweat and soften.

3 Add the cooked rice and continue to cook on a high heat, tossing occasionally, until the rice is warmed through.

4 Finally, add the soya sauce, lime juice, coriander, and spring onions. Mix and serve.

SERVES 4

jasmine rice 300g (10½oz)

sesame oil 3 tbsp

fresh root ginger 2cm (¾in) chunk, grated

garlic cloves 2, crushed

red chillies 2, finely sliced

red pepper 1, deseeded and cut into julienne strips

shiitake mushrooms 150g (5½oz), quartered

baby corn 100g (3½oz), cut into 1cm (½in) slices on the diagonal

soya sauce 3 tbsp

lime juice of 1

coriander leaves handful of, coarsely chopped

spring onions 1 bunch, finely sliced

Stuffed Vine Leaves

This is one of the first dishes that Adrian can remember cooking. It was his first day living on a communal farm in Israel, and, it being a Friday, the shops had closed early. As he sat in the garden and wondered what he might eat for dinner, he noticed a vine growing in a corner and, in a moment of inspiration and true to the spirit of our grandmother, picked some vine leaves and mint from the garden. Finding rice in the cupboard, he made this wonderful meal that was enjoyed by all.

SERVES 4

vine leaves 24

basmati rice 400g (14oz), soaked in water for 1 hour

white onion 1, finely chopped

lemons juice of 4

garlic cloves 3, crushed

mint leaves 1 bunch, finely chopped

olive oil 100ml (3½fl oz)

chopped tomatoes 1 x 400g (14oz) can

1 Preheat the oven to 170°C/325°F/gas mark 3.

2 If you are using vine leaves from a packet, wash the brine off thoroughly. If you are using fresh vine leaves, you will need to blanch them in boiling water for 10 seconds and then refresh in cold water.

3 To make the rice filling, drain the rice and mix with the onion, half the lemon juice, half the garlic, half the mint, and 2 tbsp of the olive oil.

4 To stuff the vine leaves, lay the leaves on the work surface, vein-side down, and place a ½ tbsp of rice in the centre of each. Fold over the two side edges and roll lengthways. Place on a baking tray, keeping the stuffed leaves tightly together.

5 Once the tray is full, make the sauce by blending together the canned tomatoes and the remaining lemon juice, mint, garlic, and olive oil. Pour over the vine leaves and cover the tray with foil.

6 Bake for 1 hour. Remove the foil and bake for a further 30 minutes. Serve hot.

3

Fritters and Pastries

We remember arriving in Calcutta for the first time with our father. After three weeks of shots and pills for tropical diseases and infections, we vowed to be cautious about where and what we ate. It was with some surprise that we found ourselves at 6am, having just arrived from the airport, outside a street café drinking *chai* and eating hot *samoosaks*. While our better instincts were saying that this was exactly what we were not supposed to be doing, the aromas of the spicy fritters were too great to resist.

A few tips for cooking fritters: check that the oil is sufficiently hot by slowly introducing a small piece of bread into it to see if it bubbles around and turns the bread golden. Put the fritters in the hot oil one at a time and fry them in small batches so that the temperature of the oil does not drop too low. They will also cook more evenly this way. A light sprinkling of salt immediately after frying will help maintain crispness.

Sweetcorn Fritters

These lovely Thai-food-inspired fritters are quick to prepare and taste wonderful with a clear chilli sauce (*see page* 160).

1 Place the sweetcorn and all the remaining ingredients, apart from the oil, in a blender. Pulse two or three times, but not enough to purée the mixture. Allow to stand for 15 minutes. The mixture will be quite loose.

2 Heat the oil in a heavy-based pan until almost smoking. Spoon the fritters individually into the oil and deep-fry them in batches until golden, about 3–4 minutes, turning over.

3 Drain well on kitchen paper, and serve hot.

SERVES 4

sweetcorn 4 ears, kernels removed

spring onions bunch, finely chopped

garlic clove 1, crushed

coriander leaves handful, finely chopped

ground coriander 1 tbsp

lime leaves 2, finely shredded

lime juice of 1

eggs 3 medium, beaten

plain flour 200g (7oz), sifted

vegetable oil, for deep-frying

Wasabi Potato Cakes Filled with Shiitake

Another dish that is always popular at The Gate is potato cakes, and we have made many different kinds. This recipe is inspired by Japanese cuisine, and the hot horseradish mash and sweet-flavoured shiitake make a perfect combination. We usually serve these cakes with pink ginger or pickled vegetables.

1 Peel the potatoes and chop them into even-sized pieces. Cook them in boiling water until soft, about 20 minutes, and then drain well. Add the *wasabi* powder, sesame seeds, and salt, and mix well. Allow to cool.

2 Preheat the oven to 190°C/375°F/gas mark 5. Put the mushrooms in a baking tray and drizzle with the sesame oil, soya sauce, and *mirin*. Bake for 15 minutes. Remove from the oven and allow to cool.

3 To make the potato cakes, take an 8cm (3¼in) ring or pastry cutter, and fill it halfway with potato mix, making a little dip in the centre. Place 1 tsp of the roasted mushroom filling in the centre, cover with more potato mix, and pat down firmly. The cake should be about 4cm (1½in) thick.

4 Release the cake from the ring by running a knife around the inside of it. Repeat this process for as many cakes as you require. Put the flour in a shallow bowl. Dip each potato cake in the flour.

5 Heat the oil in a frying pan and shallow-fry the potato cakes on both sides until golden. Drain on kitchen paper and serve hot.

SERVES 4

floury potatoes 1kg (2¼lb)

***wasabi* powder (Japanese horseradish)** 1 tsp

sesame seeds 2 tsp

salt pinch

plain flour 55g (2oz)

vegetable oil, for shallow-frying

FILLING

shiitake mushrooms 150g (5½oz), quartered and stalks removed

sesame oil 1 tbsp

soya sauce 1 tbsp

***mirin* (Japanese sweet rice wine)** 1 tsp

Buckwheat and Mozzarella Fritters with Plum Sauce

This recipe was brought to The Gate by Alex Visitine, our first and longest-serving employee, via his family home in the north of Italy. The main ingredients are the batter and plum sauce, which can be prepared a day or so in advance. The fritters make a colourful and comforting starter.

1 To make the batter, blend together the flours, egg, salt, and water and combine to a thick paste. Allow to stand in the fridge for 30 minutes.

2 To make the plum sauce, bring the plums, wine, sugar, and lemon juice to the boil, then simmer for 15 minutes. Pass through a sieve.

3 Heat the oil in a heavy-based pan until almost smoking. Using a fork or skewer, dip the individual pieces of mozzarella into the batter, then deep-fry for 2–3 minutes, turning. Drain on kitchen paper.

4 To serve, place three or four pieces of the deep-fried mozzarella on individual plates, and drizzle the plum sauce around them.

SERVES 4

vegetable oil 1 litre (1¾ pints), for deep-frying

mozzarella cheese 400g (14oz), cut into 2cm (¾in) cubes

BATTER

buckwheat flour 150g (5½oz)

plain flour 75g (2¾oz)

egg 1 medium

salt 1 tsp

cold water 350ml (12fl oz)

PLUM SAUCE

plums 6, stoned

red wine 1 tbsp

caster sugar 2 tbsp

lemon juice of 1

Broad Bean Falafels

One of our favourite places to forget about the world is Sinai, a desert peninsula in northern Egypt where the mountains meet the sea. Apart from the natural beauty and tranquillity of this place, the thing we look forward to most is eating these vibrant green fritters, made to this classic Egyptian recipe.

SERVES 4

dried broad (fava) beans 150g (5½oz), soaked in cold water overnight

fresh broad (fava) beans 100g (3½oz), shelled

Spanish onion 1 large, roughly chopped

coriander 1 bunch

garlic cloves 2

lemon juice of 1

garam masala 1 tbsp

cooked couscous handful, (*see page* 188), optional

vegetable oil, for deep-frying

1 Drain the dried broad beans.

2 Place all the ingredients, except for the oil and couscous, in a food processor (or ideally in a mincer), and blend to a thick paste. Allow to chill for 1 hour in the fridge.

3 Form the mixture into 2cm (¾in) round balls. *Falafels* can be unpredictable at times, depending on what type of processor or mincer has been used. If you find the mixture is breaking up, add the couscous to the mix.

4 Heat the oil in a heavy-based pan until almost smoking. Deep-fry the balls for 4–5 minutes, turning. Drain on kitchen paper, and serve hot.

Caramelized Onion and Goat's Cheese Tart

The combination of caramelized onion and goat's cheese is a real favourite at The Gate, and we have used it in many different ways. This recipe can make an elegant starter served on a bed of rocket leaves, or can be miniaturized for canapés.

1 Preheat the oven to 190°C/375°F/gas mark 5.

2 To start the filling, melt the butter in a pan. Add the onion and sauté until beginning to soften; about 5 minutes. Add the sugar and balsamic vinegar, and continue to cook until all the liquid has evaporated. Leave to cool.

3 Roll the pastry out to 1cm (½in) thickness. Cut into four rings about 10–12cm (4–4½in) in diameter. Score a ring lightly 1cm (½in) in from the outside. Brush this outer ring with beaten egg, which will allow the outside to puff up and hold the filling.

4 When the onions have cooled, divide equally between the inner rings of the tart cases. Crumble the goat's cheese over the onion, and bake for 15 minutes.

SERVES 4

puff pastry 250g (9oz)

egg 1 medium, beaten

FILLING

butter 25g (1oz)

red onions 3 large,
cut into thin crescents

caster sugar 1 tbsp

balsamic vinegar 1 tbsp

goat's cheese 75g (2¾oz)

Mushroom Filo Parcels

This mini mushroom strudel was something we learned from our great friend and mentor, the late George Chay. It makes a great starter or can be downsized to make an elegant canapé.

1 To start the filling, melt the butter in a pan, and add the garlic, leek, and mushrooms. Sauté until the mushrooms begin to sweat, then add the white wine. Continue to cook until all the liquid has evaporated from the pan and the mushrooms are lightly glazed; about 5 minutes. Set aside and allow to cool.

2 Preheat the oven to 190°C/375°F/gas mark 5.

3 Melt the 55g (2oz) butter in a small pan. Unroll the filo sheets, and lay one sheet of filo flat on the work surface. Brush with butter and lay another sheet directly on top. Cut the filo in half. Repeat this once more until you have four doubled sheets.

4 Divide the mushrooms and cheese equally among the four sheets. To make the parcel, pick up the four corners of each sheet and gather into the centre. Twist into a purse shape, then brush the outside well with the remaining melted butter.

5 Bake for 20 minutes or until the filo parcels are nicely browned.

SERVES 4

butter 55g (2oz)

filo pastry 1 x 200g (7oz) packet

FILLING

butter 25g (1oz)

garlic clove 1, crushed

leek 1 large, chopped

mixed mushrooms 450g (1lb), cut into 2mm ($^{1}/_{16}$in) thick slices

white wine splash

dolcelatte cheese 55g (2oz)

Buckwheat Blinis

Buckwheat, with its distinctive nutty flavour, is an excellent but under-used ingredient. We love cooking it both as a flour and a grain. At The Gate we usually serve these tasty little pancakes with a slice of goat's cheese and some olive tapenade.

1 Dissolve the yeast and sugar in the milk. Sift the flours and salt into a food processor bowl or mixing bowl.

2 When the yeast begins to react and bubble, add this, along with the eggs, to the flour. Blend or whisk until you have a smooth paste with no lumps. Cover and leave in a warm place until the mixture has doubled in size, about 30–40 minutes.

3 Heat a non-stick frying pan and lightly brush with olive oil. Ladle small amounts of the batter into the hot pan to make 5–6cm (2–2½in) pancakes. Cook for 1 minute on each side.

4 Keep in a warm place until ready to serve.

SERVES 4

dried yeast 1 tsp

caster sugar 2 tsp

warm milk 375ml (13fl oz)

plain flour 175g (6oz)

buckwheat flour 175g (6oz)

salt pinch

eggs medium, 2

olive oil 2 tbsp

Baby Pizzas with Pistachio Pesto and Goat's Cheese

There is nothing more enjoyable than making fresh pizza at home. It is important to roll the dough as thinly as possible.

1 To make the dough base, dissolve the yeast and sugar in 100ml (3½fl oz) of the warm water. Mix the salt and flour together separately. When the yeast begins to become active and bubbles, add it to the flour with enough of the remaining water to make a dough.

2 Knead this dough for 5–10 minutes until it is smooth. Place in an oiled bowl, cover with a clean tea-towel and put in a warm place to rise for about 1 hour.

3 While the dough is rising, make the pesto. Put the basil, garlic, and olive oil in a food processor and blend to a paste, then add the pistachio nuts. Do not allow the pistachios to purée too finely.

4 Preheat the oven to 230°C/450°F/gas mark 8.

5 When the dough has risen, punch out the air and divide into four balls. Roll out the balls into flat discs, and place on a baking tray(s). Spread the pesto over the discs, and then evenly divide the slices of goat's cheese and cherry tomatoes among them.

6 Bake for 12 minutes, and serve hot.

SERVES 4

goat's cheese 125g (4½oz), thinly sliced

cherry tomatoes 225g (8oz), thinly sliced

DOUGH BASE

dried yeast 1 tbsp

caster sugar 1 tsp

warm water 275ml (10½fl oz)

salt 1 tsp

plain flour 500g (1lb 2oz)

PISTACHIO PESTO

basil 1 bunch

garlic clove 1, crushed

olive oil 2 tbsp

pistachio nuts 75g (2¾oz) shelled

Tempura

This simple Japanese deep-fried dish is quick to prepare and can be made with almost any vegetable of your choice. At The Gate we usually serve it with a clear chilli sauce (*see page* 160). You should be able get black sesame seeds at any Asian shop; if you can't find them, use white ones instead.

1 Prepare all the vegetables shortly before cooking.

2 To make the batter, combine all the ingredients in a food processor. The batter should be thick enough to coat the vegetables but loose enough to shake off any excess.

3 Heat the oil in a heavy-based pan until almost smoking.

4 Dip the vegetables individually into the batter, then deep-fry them in batches in the hot oil until golden brown, about 3–4 minutes, turning.

5 Drain well on kitchen paper, and serve hot.

SERVES 4

red pepper 1, deseeded and cut into 2cm (¾in) wide strips

aubergine 1 small, sliced into 3mm (1/18in) thick rounds

broccoli florets 55g (2oz)

shiitake mushrooms 55g (2oz)

vegetable oil, for deep-frying

BATTER

cornflour 100g (3½oz)

plain flour 55g (2oz)

lager 80ml (2½fl oz)

black sesame seeds 1 tsp

salt 1 tsp

egg medium, 1

Wild Mushroom Pakoras

Pakoras were a Sunday afternoon treat when we were kids. Our attention would quickly be diverted from Brian Moore and the big match when these deep-fried nuggets appeared on the coffee table, usually accompanied by a coriander chutney (*see pages* 169 and 171).

1 Mix the flour with the salt, turmeric, paprika, coriander, cumin, and *ajowan* seeds. Beat in 200ml (7fl oz) water to make a thick paste, ensuring there are no lumps. Add the mushrooms, garlic, coriander leaves, and lemon juice, and bind the ingredients together. The mixture should feel quite thick. Allow to stand for 20 minutes.

2 Heat the oil in a heavy-based pan until almost smoking. Spoon in the pakoras individually and deep-fry until golden for about 4–5 minutes, turning.

3 Drain well on kitchen paper, and serve immediately.

SERVES 4

chickpea (gram) flour 55g (2oz)

salt 1 tsp

ground turmeric, **paprika**, **ground coriander**, **and ground cumin** 1 level tsp of each

ajowan or caraway seeds 1 tsp

wild mushrooms, 250g (9oz), chopped

garlic clove 1, crushed

coriander leaves handful, chopped

lemon juice of 1

vegetable oil, for deep-frying

Parmesan Biscotti with Goat's Cheese and Basil Pâté

These delightful Parmesan biscuits make elegant canapés and can accompany a variety of toppings, such as pesto and tapenade. The pastry is quick and easy to make and keeps well in the freezer to be baked at your convenience.

MAKES ABOUT 20

plain flour 200g (7oz)

butter 85g (3oz)

Parmesan 55g (2oz), freshly grated

egg yolk 1 medium

chives small bunch, for garnish

tomato 1, diced, for garnish

PÂTÉ

goat's cheese 100g (3½oz)

basil small handful of leaves

olive oil 1 tbsp

1 To make the biscuits, place the flour and butter in a food processor and combine until it resembles breadcrumbs. Add the Parmesan, egg yolk, and 1 tbsp water, and mix well to a dough. Allow to rest for 1 hour.

2 Roll out the pastry to the thickness of a £1 coin. Using a pastry cutter, cut into discs of about 5cm (2in) in diameter. Put on a baking tray lined with greaseproof paper.

3 Rest the pastry for 20 minutes, while you preheat the oven to 190°C/375°F/gas mark 5.

4 Bake the biscuits for 10–12 minutes. Watch them carefully.

5 To make the pâté, combine the goat's cheese, basil, and olive oil in a food processor.

6 To serve, put a small amount of pâté on each biscuit: use a piping bag or make tiny quenelles (balls) with a tsp. Garnish with chopped chives and tomato.

Plantain Chips

Plantains are not often found in supermarkets but you can get them in West-Indian or African shops. We often use these crispy fried slices as a tasty garnish for soups and casseroles. They are also good with *crudités,* dips, and chilli sauces.

1 Cut the plantains into slices 3–5mm ($\frac{1}{8}$–$\frac{1}{4}$in) thick.

2 Put some flour in a shallow bowl. Dip the plantain slices in the flour and reserve them on a plate.

3 Heat the oil in a heavy-based pan until almost smoking. Drop in the plantain slices in small batches at a time, and deep-fry for 3–4 minutes, until golden brown.

4 Place the chips on kitchen paper in a bowl, and sprinkle with sea salt.

SERVES 4

plantains 2 (medium-ripe), peeled

plain flour

vegetable oil, for deep-frying

sea salt, to serve

Polenta Chips

This is a great way to utilize leftover polenta – in fact, it works better if the polenta is made the day before. These chips are a popular feature of our brunch menu as a tasty surrogate for fries, served with an aïoli or chilli sauce (*see page* 160).

1 In a large pan, bring 1 litre (1¾ pints) water to the boil with the garlic, Parmesan, thyme, and butter. When boiling, slowly whisk in the polenta. The mixture should be quite thick, slowly returning to the side of the pan on stirring. Turn down the heat to very low and continue stirring the polenta with a wooden spoon for 2–3 minutes; be careful it doesn't "spit".

2 Pour the polenta mixture into an oiled shallow tray, about 25 x 20cm (10 x 8in), and smooth the top using an oiled palette knife or a rolling pin.

3 Allow the polenta to cool, then cut it into sticks of about 6 x 2cm (2½ x ¾in). Remove from the tray and lightly dust with flour.

4 Heat the oil in a heavy-based pan until almost smoking. Deep-fry the polenta chips in batches for 6–8 minutes, until crisp. Remove from the oil and place on kitchen paper.

SERVES 4

garlic clove 1, crushed

Parmesan, 55g (2oz), freshly grated

thyme pinch, chopped

butter 55g (2oz)

"pronto" or quick-cook polenta 250g (9oz)

plain flour, for dusting

vegetable oil, for deep-frying

Butternut and Cashew Samoosaks

We particularly enjoy this recipe because the natural sweetness of the butternut complements the spices and gives the dish a lovely balance of flavours. The filo pastry casing is excellent either baked or shallow-fried.

1 Preheat the oven to 200°C/400°F/gas mark 6. Dice the butternut squash and mix with 1 tbsp of the vegetable oil. Bake on a baking tray for 15–20 minutes. Remove from the oven, and turn the temperature up to 220°C/425°F/gas mark 7 to preheat for the *samoosaks*.

2 While the butternut squash is roasting, heat the remaining oil in a pan. Add the turmeric and garam masala, quickly followed by the garlic, onion, and ginger. Turn the heat down and cook together for 10–15 minutes until all the excess water from the onion has evaporated. Add the tamarind paste and sugar. When the butternut squash is cooked, mix into the mixture, along with the drained cashews and coriander. Leave to cool.

3 To make the *samoosaks*, take one sheet of filo and brush with oil. Place another sheet directly on top, and cut the filo into strips about 8cm (3¼in) wide. Place 1 tbsp filling at the bottom corner of the strip. Fold the pastry over the filling to make a triangular shape. Maintaining the triangular shape, keep folding the pastry over itself to the top. You should make about six *samoosaks*.

4 Place the *samoosaks* on a baking sheet, brush with oil, and bake for 15 minutes.

SERVES 4–6

filo pastry 1 x 200g (7oz) packet

vegetable oil 100ml (3½fl oz)

FILLING

butternut squash 400g (14oz), peeled and deseeded

vegetable oil 3 tbsp

turmeric 1 tsp

garam masala 1 tbsp

garlic clove 1, crushed

small onion 1, grated

fresh root ginger 1 x 2cm (¾in) piece, grated

tamarind paste 1 tsp

caster sugar 1 tsp

cashew nuts 100g (3½oz), soaked in boiling water for 10 minutes

coriander leaves handful, chopped

Dhania (Coriander) Chutney Sandwiches

We call these sarnies the Indian version of the chip butty, and they may well be among the first fusion dishes ever created. The combination of sliced bread (which in India is something of a delicacy), coriander chutney, and mashed potato is delicious and moreish. We remember these as real favourites at family gatherings when we were growing up: a plate of green sandwiches never lasted long.

SERVES 4

floury potatoes 1kg (2¼lb), peeled

white sliced bread 1 large loaf

DHANIA (CORIANDER) CHUTNEY

coriander 1 bunch

green chillies 2

garlic clove 1

salt 1 tsp

lemons juice of 2

1 Boil the potatoes for about 20 minutes or until tender. Mash and leave to cool.

2 While the potatoes are cooking, make the chutney. Place the coriander (leaves and stalks), chillies, garlic, salt, and lemon juice in a blender with enough water to allow it to become a smooth paste.

3 When the potatoes are cool, pour in the coriander chutney and mash in well.

4 Spread the green potato filling thickly on a slice of bread and top with another slice. Trim off the crusts. Repeat the process until you have run out of filling.

4

Spicy Dishes

When we were growing up in our Indo-Iraqi family, chilli was a common ingredient in much of our food. We can never forget the curries that our grandmother prepared, with their mouth- and eye-watering aromas and flavours; they were so hot that we could only eat a few spoonfuls with a large bowl of cooling rice.

So it is no surprise that spicy food and chillies have played a large part in our menus at The Gate. When we first started cooking and opened the restaurant, most of our dishes were quite spicy. It was only when we came to understand that not everyone wanted to eat spicy foods all the time that we began to explore and appreciate more subtle flavours. All the dishes in this chapter feature chilli and spices, but the chillies are used as much to intensify the flavours of other ingredients as for their unique flavour and heat. Chilli and spices give food the intensity we love, as well as invigorating and warming the palate.

Massaman Curry

This curry traditionally comes from southern Thailand, where the food is influenced by Malaysian cuisine. The pungent array of spices serves as a perfect combination with the sweet potato and pak-choi, and is usually served with jasmine rice. You could double the curry paste recipe; it keeps well in the fridge.

SERVES 4

coconut milk 800ml (28fl oz)

baby corn 150g (5½oz), cut into 2cm (¾in) pieces

mange-tout 100g (3½oz)

sweet potatoes 100g (3½oz), peeled and cut into 1cm (½in) slices

pak-choi 2 heads, coarsely chopped

CURRY PASTE

garlic cloves 2, roughly chopped

fresh root ginger 2cm (¾in) chunk, grated

green chillies 3, roughly chopped

lemon grass stalks 2, outer layers removed, roughly chopped

fresh *galangal* (*see page* 187), 2cm (¾in) piece, grated

ground cloves 1 tsp

ground cinnamon 1 tsp

star anise 1, crushed

caster sugar 3 tbsp

1 To make the curry paste, place all the ingredients in a food processor and blend well, adding a few drops of water to help the blending process.

2 Put the coconut milk and curry paste in a large pan and bring to the boil. Simmer for 20 minutes.

3 Add the vegetables to the curry sauce, and simmer for a further 10 minutes.

Green Thai Curry

This recipe appears to have a long ingredients list, but it is very simple to prepare. It is worth making a double batch of the curry paste because it will remain fresh in the fridge or freezer for months.

1 To make the paste, blend all the ingredients together in a food processor, adding a few drops of water to help the blending process.

2 In a pan, mix the curry paste with the coconut milk and bring to the boil. Simmer for 20 minutes.

3 Add the vegetables to the curry sauce and simmer for a further 15 minutes.

SERVES 4

coconut milk 800ml (28fl oz)

baby corn 150g (5½oz), cut into 2cm (¾in) pieces

French beans 75g (2¾oz), topped, tailed, and halved

shiitake mushrooms 75g (2¾oz)

white baby aubergines (or ordinary aubergines), 100g (3½oz)

GREEN THAI CURRY PASTE

Thai shallots 55g (2oz), roughly chopped

lemon grass stalks 2, outer layers removed, roughly chopped

lime leaves 3

garlic cloves 3, roughly chopped

fresh root ginger 2cm (¾in) chunk, grated

fresh *galangal* (*see page* 187) 2cm (¾in) chunk, grated

green chillies 3, roughly chopped

coriander 1 bunch

caster sugar 1 tbsp

soya sauce 1 tbsp

Thai Potato Cakes

Potato cakes are one of the ultimate comfort foods. They are versatile and can be enjoyed by themselves or as part of a larger dish. This recipe was inspired by an aunt, who used to make potato cakes very similar to these when we were young.

1 Boil, peel, and mash the potatoes and leave to cool.

2 When the mash is cold, mix it with the spring onion, fresh and ground coriander, lime juice, and lemon grass.

3 Mould into cakes by hand or use a pastry cutter to make rounds of about 7.5cm (3in).

4 Roll the potato cakes in flour and shallow-fry for 3–4 minutes on each side. Drain on kitchen paper and serve hot.

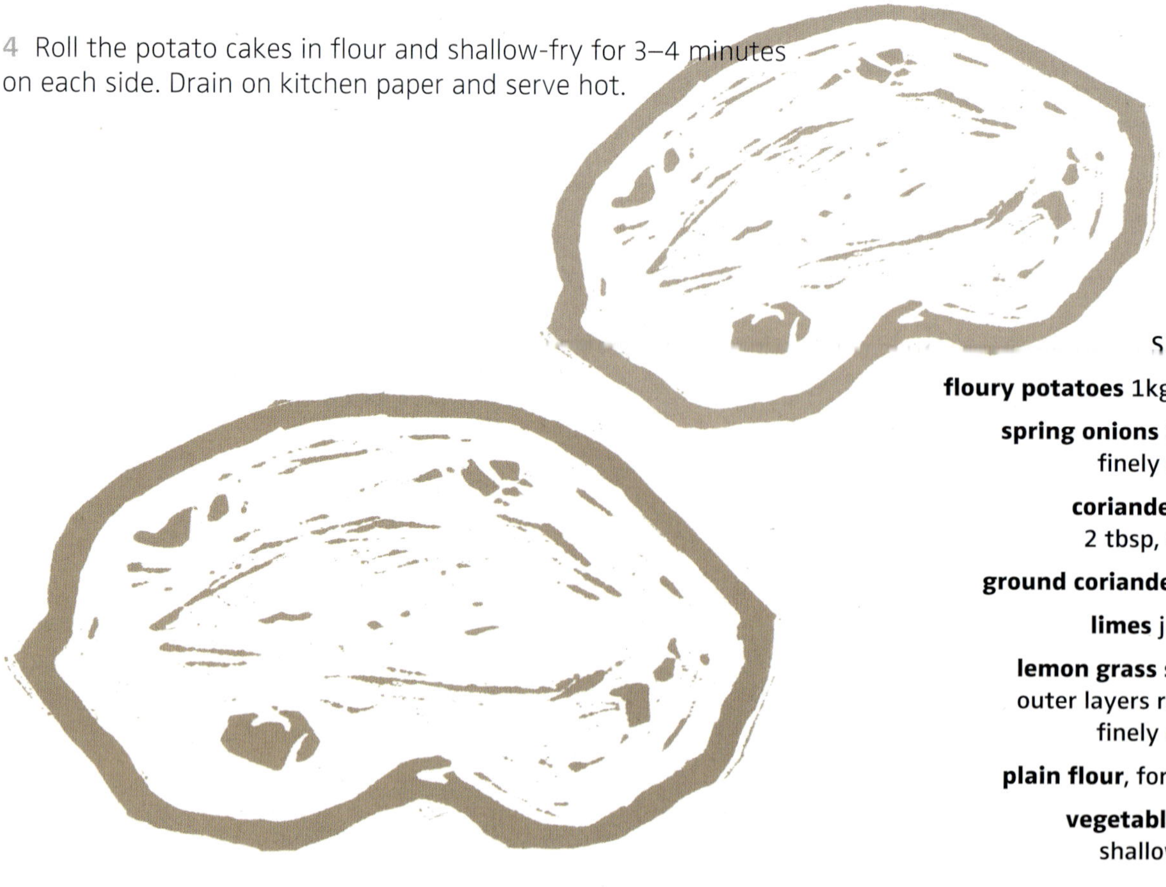

SERVES 4

floury potatoes 1kg (2¼lb)

spring onions 1 bunch, finely chopped

coriander leaves 2 tbsp, chopped

ground coriander 1 tbsp

limes juice of 2

lemon grass stalks 2, outer layers removed, finely chopped

plain flour, for dusting

vegetable oil, for shallow-frying

Baked Couscous Aubergine

We remember sitting in a menu meeting with the chefs at The Gate and talking about creating a new recipe with the taste and flavours of the Middle East. We did this by making a *chermoula,* a classic Middle Eastern marinade of herbs and spices, which we combined with curd cheese. At The Gate we usually serve this dish with Chickpea and Beetroot Salad and Harissa chilli sauce (*see pages* 135 and 161).

SERVES 4

couscous 150g (5½oz)

turmeric 1 tsp

aubergines 2 medium

egg 1 medium, beaten

CHERMOULA FILLING

olive oil 2 tbsp

cumin seeds 1 tsp, toasted in a hot dry pan for 1 minute

red onion 1, thinly sliced

garlic clove 1, crushed

red chillies 2, finely chopped

curd cheese (or cream cheese), 100g (3½oz)

flaked almonds 75g (2¾oz), toasted in a hot dry pan for 1 minute

pickled lemon 1, finely chopped

1 Put the couscous in a pan with the turmeric, pour in enough boiling water just to cover, cover with cling film, and set aside to soak and absorb for 30 minutes.

2 Preheat the grill to a high temperature, and preheat the oven to 220°C/425°F/gas mark 7.

3 Cut the aubergines lengthways into eight 3mm (⅛in) thick slices. Grill on both sides until slightly spongy and soft.

4 To make the *chermoula* filling, heat the olive oil in a medium pan. Add the cumin seeds, onion, garlic, and chilli and sauté for 5–6 minutes until the onion is soft. Remove from the heat and fold in the curd cheese, almonds, and pickled lemon.

5 To assemble, spread each of four slices of aubergine with 2 tbsp *chermoula*. Cover with another slice of aubergine and lightly compress. Dip the aubergine "sandwich" into the beaten egg and coat with the couscous.

6 Place on a baking tray and bake for 15–20 minutes. Serve hot.

Wild Mushrooms in Chipotle Sour Cream

This recipe is really a stroganoff on heat. The smoky flavour of the *chipotle* chillies enlivens the sour cream sauce. Our favourite way to eat this dish is with a simple mash or roasted potatoes.

1 In a pan, melt the butter and sweat the onion with the *chipotle* purée and paprika for 3–4 minutes.

2 Add the wild mushrooms and white wine, and continue to cook until the excess water and wine have almost completely reduced: about 6–7 minutes.

3 Stir in the sour cream and simmer for 4–5 minutes. Add the chives and serve hot.

SERVES 4

butter 55g (2oz)

red onion 1 large, thinly sliced

***chipotle* chilli** 1, puréed

paprika 1 tsp (smoked would be good)

wild mushrooms 750g (1lb 10oz), cleaned, and sliced if large

white wine dash

sour cream 300ml (10fl oz)

chives 1 bunch, finely chopped

Chat'Patay

A kind of chilli con carne, this dish is a traditional roadside snack in India. The tamarind provides a lovely tangy flavour and creates the sauce for the chickpeas and potatoes. When we were children, there was always a pot of this stew simmering in our kitchen on Bonfire Night.

1 Boil the potato for 7–8 minutes and drain well.

2 Heat the oil in a medium saucepan. Add the cumin, coriander, ginger, and onion and cook for 3–4 minutes.

3 Dissolve the tamarind paste in 100ml (3½fl oz) boiling water.

4 Add the potato, chickpeas, salt, and tamarind stock to the spices and cook for 10–15 minutes on a low heat before serving.

SERVES 4

waxy potatoes 4 large, cut into 2cm (¾in) cubes

vegetable oil 1 tbsp

ground cumin and coriander 1 tbsp of each

fresh root ginger 2cm (¾in) chunk, grated

red onion 1, finely chopped

cooked chickpeas 800g (1¾lb)

salt 1 tsp

tamarind paste 1 tbsp

Korma

Although it is not a dish that we traditionally cook at home, korma – with its sweet spices and yogurt – has more of a delicate flavour than most Indian curries, and has proved a popular dish at The Gate. We serve it with complementary sweet vegetables such as pumpkin and Jerusalem artichokes.

SERVES 4

Jerusalem artichokes 100g (3½oz), blanched

cauliflower 150g (5½oz), cut into florets

pumpkin flesh 100g (3½oz), cut into 2.5cm (1in) cubes

KORMA SAUCE

garlic cloves 2, roughly chopped

fresh root ginger 2cm (¾in) chunk, grated

red chillies 3, roughly chopped

Spanish onion 1 small, roughly chopped

vegetable oil 1 tbsp

turmeric 1 tsp

garam masala 1 tbsp

ground coriander 1 tbsp

black mustard seeds 1 tsp

cardamom pods 4, crushed

coconut milk 800ml (28fl oz)

ground almonds 55g (2oz)

natural yogurt 100g (3½oz)

1 For the sauce, blend together the garlic, ginger, chillies, and onion in a food processor.

2 Heat the oil in a pan then add the turmeric, garam masala, ground coriander, mustard seeds, and cardamom pods. Fry the spices in the hot oil for a minute or so, then add the blended onion mix and cook on a medium heat for 6–7 minutes, turning constantly.

3 Once most of the moisture has evaporated, add the coconut milk and ground almonds. Bring to the boil and simmer for 15 minutes.

4 Add the artichokes, cauliflower, and pumpkin to the sauce, and continue to simmer for a further 15 minutes.

5 Stir in the yogurt just before serving.

Braised Pumpkin and Green Beans

The fermented soya beans in this recipe give the dish a really distinctive flavour that combines beautifully with the sweetness of the pumpkin. The beans come dried in small packets, available at Asian grocers.

1 In a large pan or wok, heat the sesame oil. Add the garlic, ginger, onion, and drained soya beans, and sauté together for 2–3 minutes.

2 Put the soya beans and water in a blender and blend. Add to the pan along with the pumpkin and green beans, cover, and simmer for 10–12 minutes.

3 Remove the lid, add the soya sauce and *mirin*, and continue cooking for a further 2–3 minutes or until the vegetables are cooked.

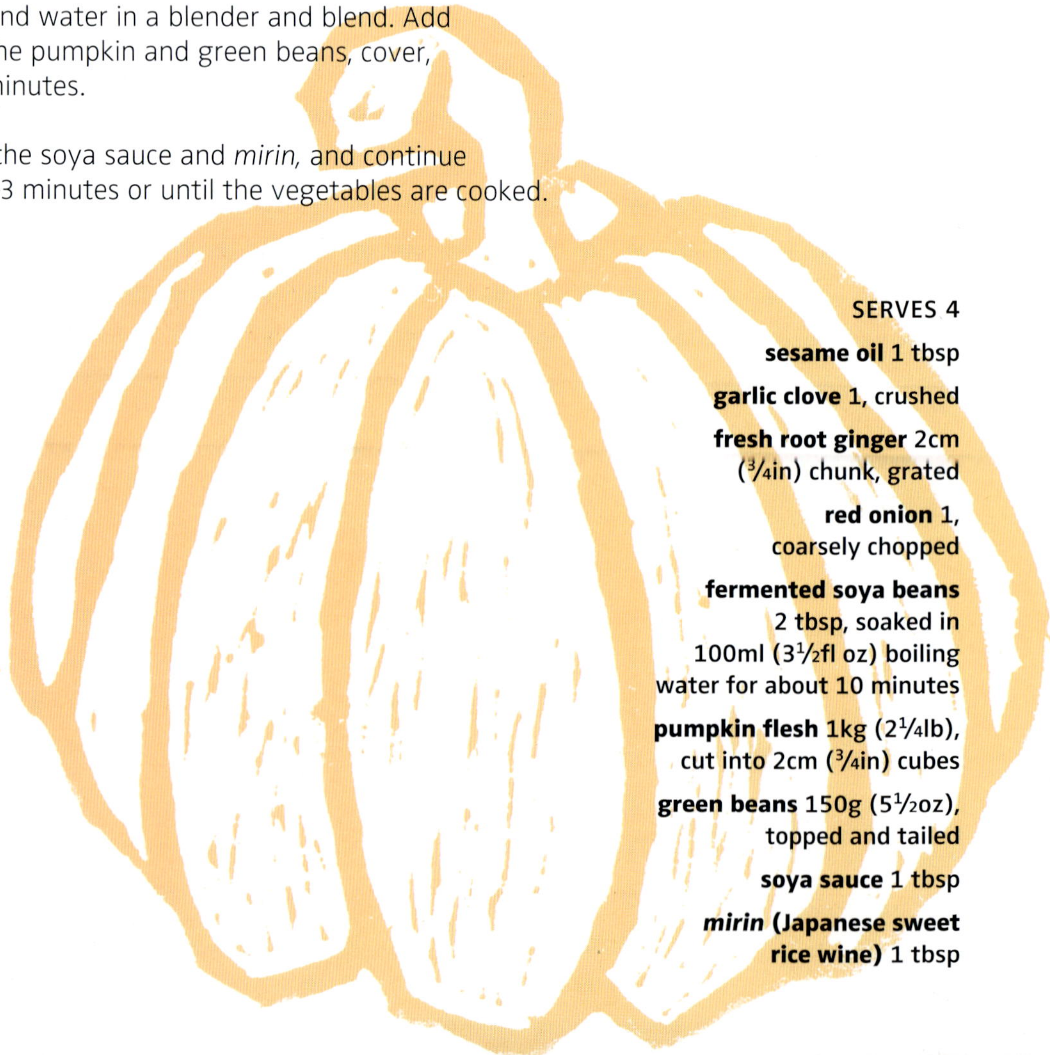

SERVES 4

sesame oil 1 tbsp

garlic clove 1, crushed

fresh root ginger 2cm (¾in) chunk, grated

red onion 1, coarsely chopped

fermented soya beans 2 tbsp, soaked in 100ml (3½fl oz) boiling water for about 10 minutes

pumpkin flesh 1kg (2¼lb), cut into 2cm (¾in) cubes

green beans 150g (5½oz), topped and tailed

soya sauce 1 tbsp

mirin **(Japanese sweet rice wine)** 1 tbsp

Portobello Mushroom and Paneer Stack

When Adrian invites our chefs over for dinner, there is a tradition that he cooks Indian food. As an alternative to the usual curries he prepares for them, this dish was created with a summer evening in mind, when a heavy curry does not appeal. *Paneer* is a mild, firm-textured Indian cheese that absorbs the flavour of spices. This mushroom and *paneer* dish with its spicy dauphinoise is both comforting and elegant.

SERVES 4

Portobello mushrooms 4 large, stalks removed

olive oil 1 tbsp

***paneer* cheese** 150g (5½oz), finely diced

red onion 1, finely diced

red chilli 1, finely diced

coriander leaves 1 bunch, finely chopped

lemon juice of 1

SPICY DAUPHINOISE

potatoes 5 large

double cream 100ml (3½fl oz)

garam masala 1 tbsp

1 Preheat the oven to 190°C/375°F/gas mark 5.

2 To make the spicy dauphinoise, peel the potatoes then slice them on a mandoline to 2mm (1/16in) thickness. Mix the double cream with the garam masala. Grease a 30 x 23cm (12 x 9in) baking tray with a little of the dauphinoise cream. Lay the potato slices on the baking tray, brushing with cream between each layer (and using it all up). Cover with foil and bake for 40 minutes.

3 Meanwhile, brush the mushrooms with olive oil and bake alongside the potato for 15 minutes.

4 To make a filling for the mushrooms, mix together the *paneer*, onion, chilli, coriander, and lemon juice.

5 Once the mushrooms are cool enough to handle, divide the *paneer* mix among them and bake for a further 10 minutes along with the potato.

6 Serve the mushrooms on top of the potato bake.

Chipotle Artichokes with Feta and Avocado

Chipotles are small, hot Mexican chillies with an intense smokiness that works well here with the subtle flavours of artichoke and avocado. Remember to prepare the avocado just before cooking to prevent it from browning, but the artichokes can be prepared a day or so in advance if kept in water to which a spot of lemon juice or vinegar has been added (you could also poach them in advance). Should you want to avoid the job of preparing them yourself, peeled frozen artichoke hearts are available in many supermarkets.

1 Preheat the oven to 200°C/400°F/gas mark 6.

2 Prepare the artichokes by peeling off all the leaves down to the heart and removing the hairy "choke". Poach the hearts in a pot of water with the juice of 1 lemon and the chillies for 10–12 minutes.

3 While the artichokes are cooking, mix the avocado, feta cheese, spring onion, coriander, remaining lemon juice, and sun-dried tomato in a bowl. Drain the artichokes.

4 When the artichokes have softened, refresh in cold water, and divide the avocado stuffing among them.

5 Bake for 12 minutes and serve hot.

SERVES 4

globe artichokes 4

lemons juice of 2

***chipotle* chillies** 2

avocados 2, stoned, peeled, and diced

feta cheese 100g (3½oz), cubed

spring onions 6, finely chopped

coriander leaves 1 tbsp, chopped

sun-dried tomatoes 25g (1oz), cut into strips

5

Side Dishes

In contrast to European cooking, where meals are often based around one main dish, Asian meals tend to comprise a number of smaller side dishes, especially in our home.

This has influenced our cooking at The Gate. Many of our main courses are actually a number of side dishes combined on one plate. It is in this spirit that this chapter came to be.

Often when we are shopping for a dinner party, a particular vegetable will catch the eye and we will want to cook it for our guests in addition to the other dishes we have planned. The recipes in this chapter are predominantly single-vegetable dishes, and simple techniques for cooking them bring out their best flavour and texture.

Marinated Baby Artichokes

Probably because they look like flowers, artichokes are among the most visually pleasing and elegant of vegetables. Baby artichokes come into season in midsummer, and this relatively quick recipe is an excellent way to prepare and marinate them. Prepared thus, they will keep in the fridge for months, and the flavoured olive oil you have baked and stored them in will make an excellent oil for salads.

SERVES 4

baby artichokes 12

olive oil 1 litre (1¾ pints)

garlic 1 bulb, skin on, halved horizontally

red chillies 2

rosemary 3 sprigs

salt 1 tbsp

lemons 2, quartered

1 To prepare the artichokes, peel off two outer layers of leaves and discard. Trim the top third of the leaves and discard. Using a vegetable peeler, peel the outer layer of skin from the base of the leaves to the bottom of the stem.

2 In a heavy-based pan, heat the oil to a medium heat. Add the garlic bulb halves, chillies, rosemary, salt, and 4 of the lemon quarters.

3 Cut the artichokes in half and rub the inner side with the lemon pieces that you have left over to avoid discoloration.

4 Add the artichokes to the infusing hot oil and slow-cook for 25 minutes or until the artichokes are soft enough to pass a knife through.

5 Leave the artichokes to cool in the oil, then decant the artichokes and oil into a sterilized jar and store in the fridge. They will keep for three or four months.

Aloo-Makalla

These are probably the best deep-fried potatoes you will ever eat. We have eaten this dish every Friday night since we can remember, and we still want more. When we were kids, our mother needed to hide the leftover *aloos* (as we call them) after Friday-night dinner, because they taste even better the next day and are traditionally eaten as part of a salad with roasted eggs and fresh chilli. However, one of us boys would come down in the middle of the night to have a little munch – they were that good. This inevitably led to questions and denial on Saturday morning. For the slightly more health-conscious, if you don't want to deep-fry these potatoes, they are just as good drizzled with oil and roasted.

1 Peel, wash, and cut the potatoes into quarters. Place in cold water to cover, add the salt and turmeric, and bring to the boil. When the water reaches boiling point, remove the potatoes immediately and drain in a colander for 10 minutes.

2 In a wok or large, deep pan, heat the oil until nearly smoking and carefully add the potatoes, one or so at a time to prevent the fat from spitting. Cook the potatoes for 7–8 minutes, then turn down the heat to moderately low and simmer for 30 minutes.

3 Turn the heat up again, and cook for a further 7–8 minutes until the potatoes are a golden brown colour.

SERVES 4

King Edward potatoes 1kg ($2\frac{1}{4}$lb – about 4 large)

salt and turmeric 1 tsp of each

vegetable oil 1 litre ($1\frac{3}{4}$ pints), for deep-frying

Deep-fried Kumara

Kumara, the traditional Maori name for sweet potato, is a real favourite of all the Kiwi chefs who have passed through The Gate. The striking colour of these crisps makes them a beautiful garnish, and they're also great munched on their own.

1 Using a vegetable peeler, peel the sweet potatoes, then cut thin strips off them all around.

2 Heat the oil to medium in a wok or large, deep pan.

3 Deep-fry a handful of these strips at a time, remembering to keep them moving in the oil to prevent them from sticking together and burning.

4 Drain well on kitchen paper and sprinkle with sea salt.

SERVES 4

sweet potatoes 2 red

vegetable oil 1 litre ($1\frac{3}{4}$ pints), for deep-frying

sea salt flakes 1 tbsp

Caramelized Fennel

Growing up as a fussy eater was not easy for Adrian – or for our mother. When we started to cook, we made it our goal to discover vegetables and the best way of cooking them. Fennel is one of those vegetables that people love or hate. This is probably our favourite way of eating it because the caramelization with the butter and white wine brings out fennel's delicate sweetness, and it is a perfect accompaniment to a plate of wild mushrooms with a few sautéed potatoes.

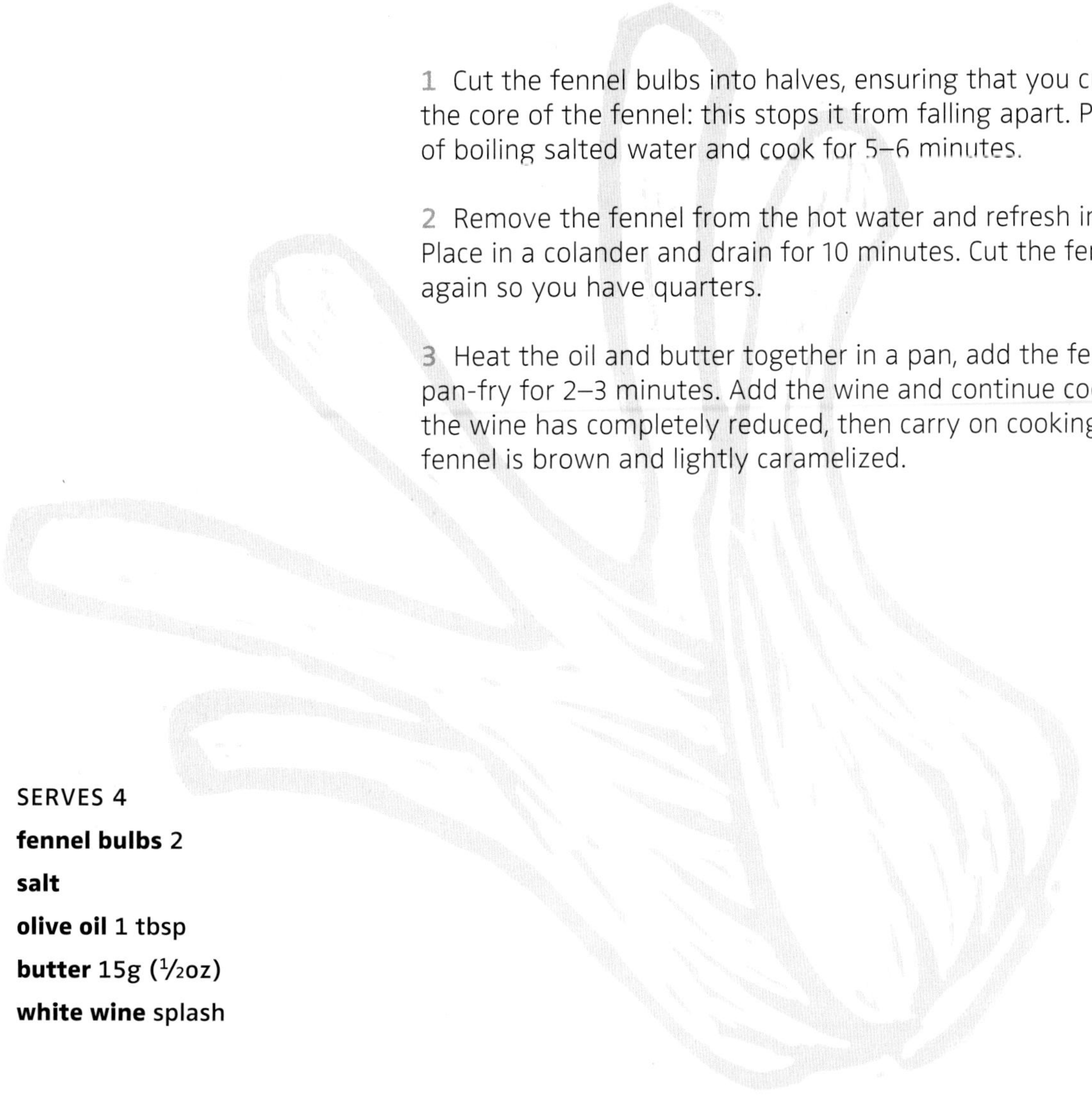

1 Cut the fennel bulbs into halves, ensuring that you cut through the core of the fennel: this stops it from falling apart. Place in a pan of boiling salted water and cook for 5–6 minutes.

2 Remove the fennel from the hot water and refresh in cold water. Place in a colander and drain for 10 minutes. Cut the fennel in half again so you have quarters.

3 Heat the oil and butter together in a pan, add the fennel, and pan-fry for 2–3 minutes. Add the wine and continue cooking until the wine has completely reduced, then carry on cooking until the fennel is brown and lightly caramelized.

SERVES 4

fennel bulbs 2

salt

olive oil 1 tbsp

butter 15g (½oz)

white wine splash

Caramelized Baby Onions

These sweetened baby onions are a great way to add bursts of flavour to dishes such as pasta and tarts, or just as an accompaniment to a meal.

1 Peel the onions: a quick technique is to cover them with boiling water. When the water has cooled, the skin will blister and remove easily.

2 In a pan, heat the baby onions, butter, and olive oil, then sprinkle with a little salt, and slowly sauté for 8–10 minutes on a medium heat.

3 Once the onions have softened, add the vinegar and sugar, and continue to cook on a low heat for a further 10–12 minutes until the vinegar has reduced into the onions.

SERVES 4

baby onions 200g (7oz)

butter 35g (1¼oz)

olive oil 1 tbsp

salt

balsamic vinegar 3 tbsp

muscovado sugar
3 tbsp light

Savoy Cabbage with Caraway Seeds

Cabbage is one of those vegetables that has really taken us a while to enjoy eating. Toasting the caraway seeds and the light pan-frying makes it a tasty accompaniment.

1 Heat a large pan and lightly toast the caraway seeds for 1 minute.

2 Add the butter and olive oil to the pan, allow to melt, and then add the cabbage. Stir the cabbage to prevent it from burning, and sauté for 3–4 minutes.

3 Add the white wine and continue to cook until the cabbage has wilted. Season with salt and pepper, add the lemon juice, and serve.

SERVES 4

caraway seeds 1 tbsp

butter 35g (1¼oz)

olive oil 1 tbsp

Savoy cabbage 1 small, cored and finely shredded

white wine splash

salt and black pepper

lemon juice of ¼

Pan-fried Samphire

Samphire, although often considered a seaweed, actually grows in grassy areas along the coasts, and is quite common in parts of Norfolk. It is available in late spring and early summer, and is usually found in fishmongers' shops.

1 Bring a pan of water to the boil.

2 In a large pan, melt the butter and add the lemon juice.

3 Blanch the samphire in the boiling water for 30 seconds and allow to drain before placing it in the pan with the butter and lemon juice. Cook, stirring, for 2–3 minutes.

4 Add the chives and serve.

SERVES 4

butter 55g (2oz)

lemon juice of 1

samphire 200g (7oz)

chives 1 tbsp, chopped

Pan-fried Kale

Kale is a member of the cabbage family, and is available throughout the winter. We were introduced to this vegetable by our good friend Ahmed, chef and owner of what was Granita. This quick and simple method of cooking kale brings out the best of its flavour and texture.

1 In a wok or large pan, heat the olive oil. Add the kale and pan-fry for 3–4 minutes, turning regularly.

2 As the kale is beginning to wilt, add the lemon juice and cook for a further minute. Season to taste, and serve immediately.

SERVES 4

olive oil 1 tbsp

kale 100g (3½oz), chopped

lemon juice of ¼

salt and black pepper

Root Vegetable Dauphinoise

This is a variation on a popular theme. The slow roasting brings out the natural sweetness of these vegetables and, layered together, they make a colourful and tasty dish.

1 Preheat the oven to 180°C/350°F/gas mark 4. Grease a 15 x 20cm (6 x 8in) baking tray with a little of the melted butter.

2 Peel all the vegetables and slice on a mandoline to a 2mm (1⁄16in) thickness.

3 Arrange a layer of potatoes flat in the baking tray, overlapping each other. Brush with melted butter and sprinkle with salt and thyme. Add another layer of potatoes, followed by three layers of carrots, seasoning each layer with salt and thyme and brushing with melted butter. Finally, top with two layers of celeriac, seasoning in between again and brushing with butter.

4 Cover the tray with foil and bake for 40 minutes. Remove the foil and bake for a further 10 minutes.

SERVES 4

butter 300g (10½oz), melted

floury potatoes 2 large

carrots 2 large

celeriac 1 small head

salt

chopped thyme 2 tbsp

Honey-roasted Parsnips

Parsnip is one of our favourite root vegetables, and this lovely technique for caramelizing works particularly well. It is a favourite on our Christmas menu.

1 Preheat the oven to 200°C/400°F/gas mark 6.

2 Toss the cut parsnips with the olive oil and thyme in a baking tray. Sprinkle with a little salt.

3 Bake for 25–30 minutes or until the parsnips are just beginning to soften.

4 Drizzle the honey over the parsnips and bake for a further 10 minutes, shaking the tray occasionally.

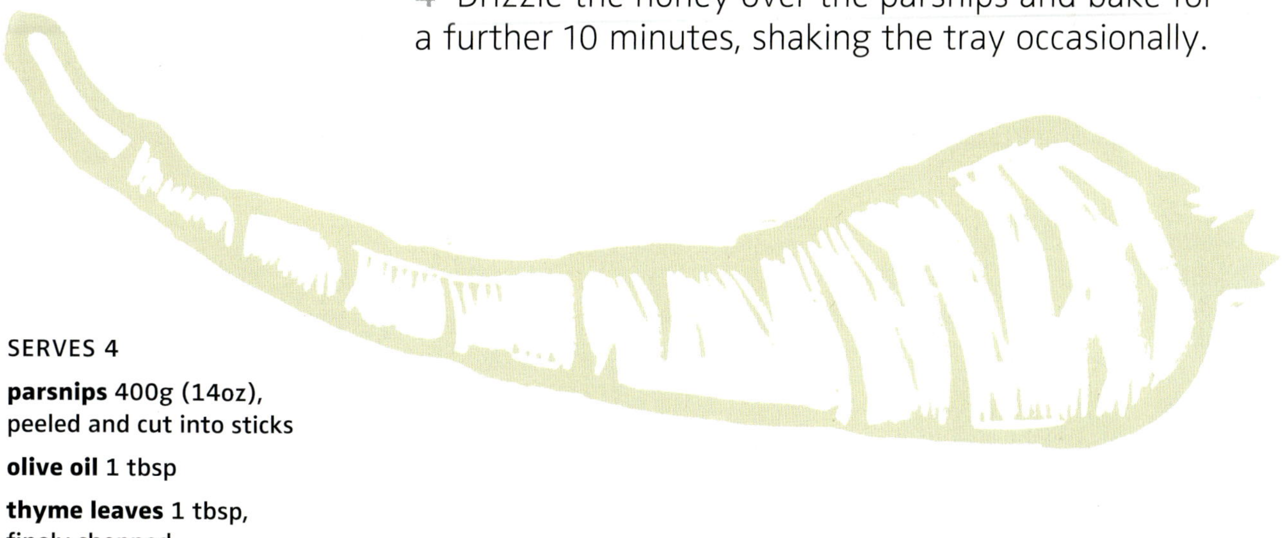

SERVES 4

parsnips 400g (14oz), peeled and cut into sticks

olive oil 1 tbsp

thyme leaves 1 tbsp, finely chopped

salt

runny honey 2 tbsp

Roast Pumpkin and Chilli

This lovely and very simple method of roasting pumpkins, skin and all, makes a great side dish.

1 Preheat the oven to 220°C/425°F/gas mark 7.

2 Toss all the ingredients together in a bowl.

3 Roast on a baking tray for 20 minutes.

SERVES 4

pumpkin 1 small, cut into 3cm ($1\frac{1}{4}$in) thick wedges, deseeded

chilli flakes 1 tbsp dried

salt 1 tsp

thyme leaves 1 tsp chopped

olive oil 1 tbsp

Horseradish Mash

Horseradish, with its nasal heat, has become very popular at The Gate, and we serve it in several different ways. This simple twist on conventional mash is a good way to enliven a meal.

1 Boil the potatoes in salted water for 10–12 minutes or until cooked.

2 Drain them well for 4–5 minutes before mashing or passing through a mouli.

3 Add the butter, add the horseradish and lemon juice, and mix well. Season to taste and serve hot.

SERVES 4

Maris Piper or other floury potatoes, 500g (1lb 2oz), peeled and cut into 2cm (3/4in) cubes

salt and black pepper

butter 40g (1 1/2oz)

fresh horseradish 75g (2 3/4oz), grated

lemon juice 1 tsp

Butternut and Rosemary Mash

Butternut is probably the prince of squashes due to its low water content and delicate, sweet flavour. It combines beautifully with rosemary and, as a side dish, is a good accompaniment to wild mushroom dishes.

1 Put the butternut squash, potato, carrot, and rosemary in a large pan. Cover with water, bring to the boil, and simmer for 10–12 minutes.

2 Drain well for 4–5 minutes, then remove the rosemary and pass through a mouli, or mash by hand.

3 Melt the butter into the mash, season with salt and pepper, and stir to mix. Serve hot.

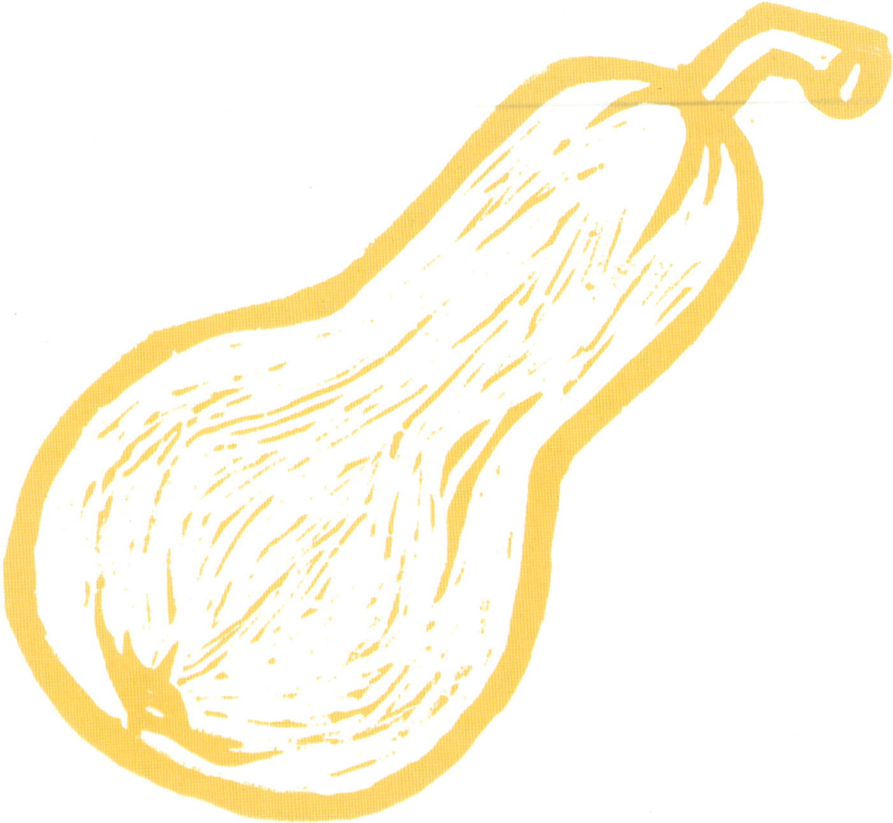

SERVES 4

butternut squash 1 medium, peeled, seeded, cut into 2cm (3/4in) cubes

Maris Piper or other floury potatoes 2, about 300g (10 1/2oz), peeled and cut into 2cm (3/4in) cubes

carrot 1 medium, peeled and cut into 2cm (3/4in) cubes

rosemary 2 sprigs

butter 75g (2 3/4oz)

salt and black pepper

6

Soups

We remember hearing a lovely fable about an old man who was given shelter by an old lady on condition that he ask for nothing. He took two small pebbles – his "magic stones" – from his bag and placed them in a pan of boiling water. As the pot simmered, he tasted the broth, turned to his companion, and said the stones were a little old and could she spare him some salt and pepper to increase the flavour? She agreed that it was not too much to ask for. He added them to the pot, tasted the soup again and said, "Mmm, much improved," and then asked if he might use a bay leaf that was on the shelf. The woman agreed, and also offered a few vegetables. Soon, the man removed the stones from the soup and the two ate. Finishing, the lady complimented her visitor and asked how two stones could make such a lovely meal!

For some reason, we never forgot this simple story from our youth. It perfectly illustrates the alchemy of soup-making and the joy of hospitality.

Kale and Cannellini Bean Soup

Bean soup has a legendary status in Middle Eastern cuisine. This soup is inspired by the classic bean soups found in the Yemenite restaurants in Jerusalem.

SERVES 4

olive oil 1 tbsp

garlic clove 1, chopped

chopped thyme 1 tsp

red onion 1 large, finely diced

celery stalk 1, finely chopped

carrot 1, peeled and finely diced

tomatoes 4, skinned and chopped

kale 100g (3½oz), shredded

cannellini beans 200g (7oz), cooked

vegetable stock 1 litre (1¾ pints), (*see page* 189)

1 Heat the oil in a large saucepan and add the garlic and thyme, quickly followed by the onion, celery, carrot, and tomatoes. Sweat off in the pan for 6–7 minutes or until softened.

2 Add the kale, beans, and stock, bring to the boil, and simmer for 10–12 minutes.

Roasted Tomato Soup

We should probably start this introduction by admitting that, until recently, no fresh tomato had passed our lips since we were boys; like most people in this country, the thought of tomato soup was for us synonymous with the name "Heinz". It was only when we first tasted a roasted tomato that we realized what a wonderful flavour it possessed with all the moisture drawn from the fruit.

1 Preheat the oven to 180°C/350°F/gas mark 4.

2 To skin the tomatoes, score the underside lightly with a knife, then place in boiling water for 10 seconds. Transfer them immediately to cold water. The skins should now slip off easily.

3 Cut the tomatoes in half and put them face up on a baking tray with the garlic bulb. Drizzle with a little of the olive oil, sprinkle with salt, and roast for about 40 minutes.

4 Remove the tray from the oven. Trim the top end of the garlic bulb and squeeze the soft purée out into a saucepan. Add the onion and remaining olive oil, and sauté on a low temperature for about 10 minutes.

5 Add the roasted tomatoes, sun-dried tomatoes, sugar, and stock to the saucepan, mix in, and simmer for about 20 minutes.

6 Blend – but do not make it too smooth – and garnish with chopped basil.

SERVES 4–6

fresh tomatoes 1.5kg (3lb 5oz)

garlic 1 whole bulb

olive oil 3 tbsp

salt 1 tsp

red onions 2, finely diced

sun-dried tomatoes 40g ($1\frac{1}{2}$oz), puréed

caster sugar 1 tbsp

vegetable stock 1.2 litres (2 pints), (*see page* 189)

basil 1 small bunch, chopped

Spinach and Jerusalem Artichoke Soup

For people who started out not loving vegetables, the road to Damascus has been filled with some wonderful surprises, none more so than the Jerusalem artichoke. Its subtle nuttiness combines well with a variety of other vegetables and seasonings, which is illustrated beautifully in this delicious soup, with its gentle flavour and ambient colour.

1 Preheat the oven to 220°C/425°F/gas mark 7. Lightly oil the Jerusalem artichokes, place in a roasting tray, and roast for 15 minutes.

2 Sauté the leek and garlic in the remaining oil for 2–3 minutes. Add the white wine and continue to cook for a further 2–3 minutes until the liquid has reduced completely.

3 Add the Jerusalem artichokes and vegetable stock and simmer for 15 minutes.

4 Add the fresh spinach and lemon juice. Blend and serve.

SERVES 4

Jerusalem artichokes 400g (14oz), chopped into 2cm (3/4in) pieces

olive oil 2 tbsp

leek 1 large, finely diced

garlic cloves 2, crushed

white wine, splash

vegetable stock, 1.25 litres (2 pints), (*see page* 189)

fresh spinach 150g (5½oz), washed

lemon, juice of 1

Pumpkin and Jerusalem Artichoke Soup

This is one of our favourite soups, primarily because the two protagonist vegetables, while both subtle in flavour, blend beautifully together.

1 In a large saucepan, heat the oil and add the garlic and herbs, quickly followed by the onion and celery.

2 Once the ingredients have begun to sweat, add the artichokes and pumpkin. Cook for 5–6 minutes, allowing the vegetables to gain colour, then add the stock and bring to the boil.

3 Simmer for 20–25 minutes, then blend to a smooth consistency.

SERVES 4

olive oil 1 tbsp

garlic clove 1, chopped

rosemary and thyme 1 tsp of each, chopped

Spanish onions 2 large, chopped

celery stalks 3, chopped

Jerusalem artichokes 400g (14oz), peeled

pumpkin 1kg (2¼lb), peeled, deseeded, and cut into 2cm (¾in) dice

vegetable stock 1 litre (1¾ pints), (*see page* 189)

Butternut Squash Kutta

This is one of those Indo-Iraqi soupy stews that we love. This particular dish is traditional for the Jewish New Year. The sweetness of the butternut squash and sultanas combines beautifully with the piquancy of the lemon and celery. At home, rice is served with all meals, and freshly boiled rice works particularly well when served with a bowl of *kutta*.

SERVES 4–6

red onion 1 large, chopped

garlic cloves 3, crushed

fresh root ginger 2cm ($^3/_4$in) chunk, grated

turmeric 1 tsp

olive oil 1 tbsp

butternut squash 500g (1lb 2oz), peeled and deseeded, cut into 3cm ($1^1/_4$in) cubes

tomatoes 400g (14oz) (fresh or canned), chopped

sultanas handful

celery stalks 2, chopped

celery leaves handful

lemon juice of 1

mint and coriander leaves handful of each

shelled almonds 55g (2oz), toasted in a hot dry pan for 1 minute and chopped

caster sugar 1 tbsp

1 Sauté the onion, garlic, ginger, and turmeric in the oil for 3–4 minutes.

2 Add the butternut squash, tomatoes, sultanas, celery, celery leaves, and 400ml (14fl oz) water. Bring to the boil and simmer until the butternut squash is tender, about 20–25 minutes.

3 Add the lemon juice, mint and coriander, almonds, and sugar, and cook for a further 5 minutes. Serve.

Leek and Potato Soup with Cep Stock

This simple variation on leek and potato soup really benefits from the robust flavour that the dried ceps provide.

1 Soak the ceps in the water for 30 minutes. Drain well, reserving the liquid. Discard the ceps.

2 In a large saucepan, gently sauté the leek and garlic in the butter until the leek is softened; about 5–6 minutes. Add the white wine and potatoes and cook until the wine has evaporated.

3 Add the cep stock, bring to the boil, and simmer for 20 minutes until the potatoes are cooked. Purée with a hand-held blender and serve.

SERVES 4

dried ceps or *porcini* 75g (2¾oz)

boiling water 1.25 litres (2 pints)

leeks 1kg (2¼lb), finely sliced

garlic clove 1, chopped

butter 35g (1¼oz)

white wine 150ml (5fl oz)

potatoes 300g (10½oz), roughly chopped

Cauliflower and Stilton Soup

We admit that we are not the greatest fans of English food, which is a standing joke in The Gate's kitchen. When we find ourselves cooking a "traditional" English dish, someone will say, "This represents the best of British", and this soup definitely comes into that category. If there are two ingredients that complement each other perfectly, they are cauliflower and Stilton.

1 In a large saucepan, melt the butter and sauté the leek and garlic for 2–3 minutes. Add the cauliflower and potato and continue to cook for another 4–5 minutes.

2 Add the stock, bring to the boil, and simmer for 25 minutes.

3 Crumble in the Stilton and blend to a smooth consistency. Finally, add the double cream.

SERVES 4

butter 35g (1¼oz)

leeks 2, finely diced

garlic clove 1, chopped

cauliflower 1 large, chopped into small florets

potato 1 large, diced

vegetable stock 1 litre (1¾ pints), (*see page* 189)

Stilton cheese 55g (2oz)

double cream 75ml (2½fl oz)

Sweetcorn and Coconut Soup

Adrian became a real fan of corn soups when he was living in the United States in his early 20s. He particularly enjoys the subtle flavour of corn blending in with other strong flavours.

1 In a large saucepan, heat the butter and olive oil and add the thyme and garlic, quickly followed by the onion and sweetcorn. Sauté on a medium heat for 6–7 minutes, allowing the onion and corn to brown lightly and caramelize.

2 Add the sweet potato, coconut milk, nutmeg, and stock. Bring to the boil and simmer for 30 minutes.

3 Purée with a hand-held blender, finally adding the lime juice.

SERVES 4

butter 25g (1oz)

olive oil 1 tbsp

thyme 1 tsp chopped

garlic clove 1, crushed

Spanish onion 1 large, finely diced

sweetcorn 3 ears, kernels removed

white sweet potato 1, cut into 2cm ($\frac{3}{4}$in) cubes

coconut milk 800ml (28fl oz)

nutmeg pinch, freshly grated

vegetable stock 250ml (9fl oz), (*see page* 189)

lime juice of 1

Carrot and Cashew Nut Soup

This is one of the first recipes Adrian developed as a young chef. Trading as "Woody's", this was his first incarnation in the world of catering, and the Sesame Health Foods shop in Primrose Hill was his first customer. He delivered a large pot of this soup to it every Friday.

SERVES 4–6

Spanish onion 1 large, finely chopped

garlic cloves 2, finely chopped

fresh root ginger 3cm (1¼in) chunk, grated

ground coriander 1 tbsp

olive oil 2 tbsp

carrots 4 large, chopped

shelled cashew nuts 100g (3½oz), toasted in a hot dry pan for 1 minute

vegetable stock 1.25 litres (2 pints), (*see page* 189)

coriander leaves handful, chopped

1 Sauté the onion with the garlic, ginger, and ground coriander in the oil until the onion is translucent.

2 Add the carrot, cashew nuts, and vegetable stock, bring to the boil, and simmer for 30 minutes.

3 Add the coriander and purée with a hand-held blender.

Wild Mushroom and Pearl Barley Soup

This retro classic and winter warmer is almost a meal in itself. While very reminiscent of schooldays, the wild mushroom stock gives this soup an intense and grown-up flavour.

1 Soak the dried ceps in the boiling water for 30 minutes. Drain the ceps well, retaining the liquid. Discard the ceps.

2 Sauté the leek and garlic in the olive oil in a large pan for 2–3 minutes. Add the parsnip, carrot, and Portobello mushrooms and sauté for a further 5–6 minutes until the mushrooms emit their liquid and begin to soften.

3 Add the pearl barley and the wild mushroom stock and bring to the boil. Simmer on a medium heat for 30 minutes.

SERVES 4–6

dried ceps or *porcini* 75g (2¾oz)

boiling water 1.25 litres (2 pints)

leek 1, finely diced

garlic clove 1, crushed

olive oil 2 tbsp

parsnip 1, cut into 5mm (¼in) dice

carrot 1, cut into 5mm (¼in) dice

Portobello mushrooms 200g (7oz), coarsely chopped

pearl barley 100g (3½oz), rinsed well

Plantain Soup

Growing up in our home, we regularly saw many new and unusual vegetables and fruit, but travels to India and Brazil highlighted the great taste and versatility of one vegetable in particular: the plantain. This sweet-and-sour soup, with its creamy texture, is very popular at The Gate.

SERVES 4–6

Spanish onion 1, finely chopped

garlic cloves 2, crushed

red chilli 1, finely chopped

fresh root ginger 3cm (1¼in) chunk, grated

olive oil 2 tbsp

plantains 2 large, peeled and chopped

caster sugar 1 dsp

coconut milk 800ml (28fl oz)

water 500ml (18fl oz)

lime juice of 1

1 Sauté the onion, garlic, chilli, and ginger in the olive oil for 5–6 minutes until the onion is translucent.

2 Add the plantain and sugar and continue to cook on a medium heat until the plantain begins to caramelize: about 7–8 minutes.

3 Add the coconut milk and water, bring to the boil, and simmer on a medium heat for about 20 minutes.

4 Add the lime juice, and blend with a hand-held blender or in a food processor.

Laksa

Although *laksa* traditionally comes from Indonesia, this recipe is strongly influenced by Thai ingredients, with its refreshing citrous herbs and aromas. Don't be put off by the long list of ingredients; this dish is quick to prepare and, once made, the paste will keep well in the fridge or freezer.

1 Put the lemon grass, *galangal,* ginger, garlic, chilli, turmeric, ground coriander, and sugar in a blender. Blend to make a thick paste, adding a little water if required.

2 Put the paste, coconut milk, and 400ml (14fl oz) water in a large saucepan, and bring to the boil. Simmer for 20 minutes.

3 Add the lime juice, mange tout, and baby corn and cook for a further 3–4 minutes.

SERVES 4

lemon grass stalks 3, outer layers removed, thinly sliced

fresh *galangal* (*see page* 187) small 1cm (½in) chunk

fresh root ginger 2cm (¾in) chunk

garlic clove 1

red chilli 1

turmeric 1 tsp

ground coriander 2 tsp

caster sugar 1 tbsp

coconut milk 800ml (28fl oz)

limes juice of 2

mange-tout 100g (3½oz)

baby corn 100g (3½oz), sliced 1cm (½in) thick on the diagonal

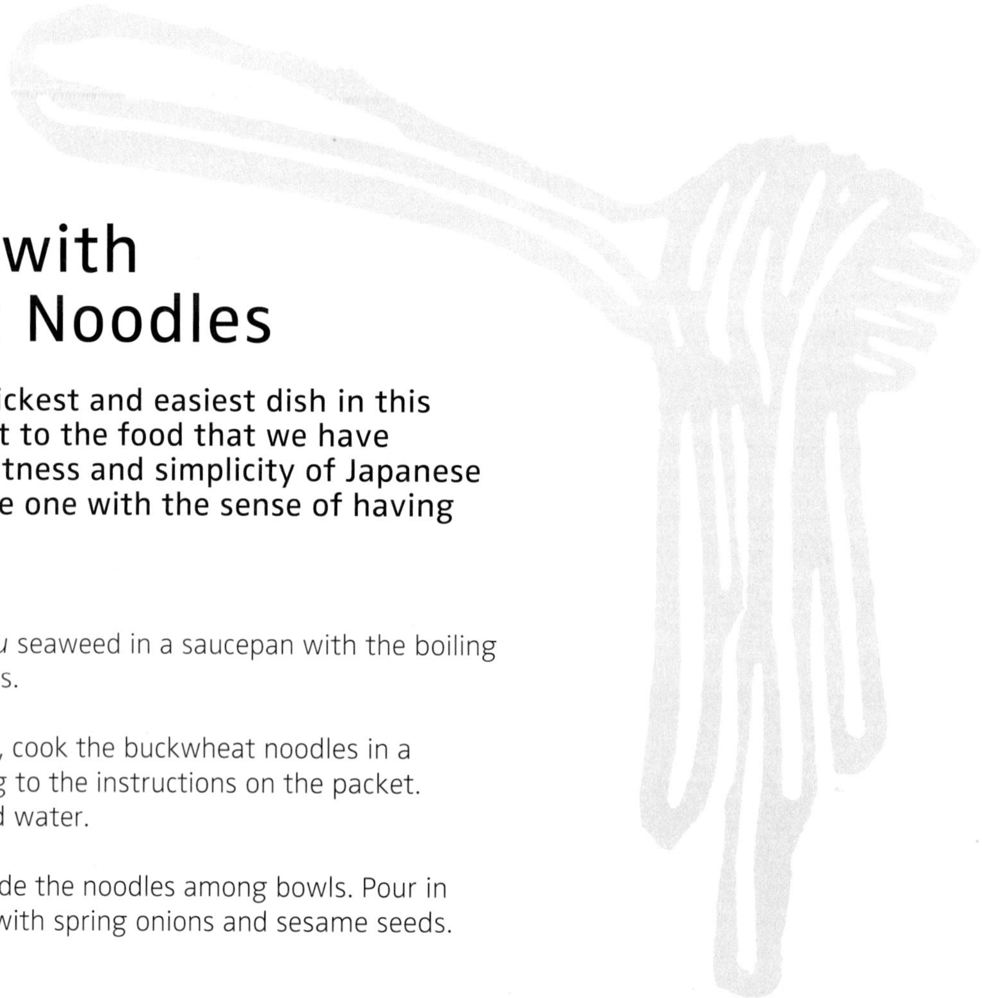

Miso Soup with Buckwheat Noodles

This is probably the quickest and easiest dish in this section, and, in contrast to the food that we have grown up with, the lightness and simplicity of Japanese cuisine can almost leave one with the sense of having forgotten something.

1 Place the *miso* and *kombu* seaweed in a saucepan with the boiling water and boil for 15 minutes.

2 While the *miso* is cooking, cook the buckwheat noodles in a separate saucepan according to the instructions on the packet. When cooked, refresh in cold water.

3 When ready to serve, divide the noodles among bowls. Pour in the *miso* stock and garnish with spring onions and sesame seeds.

SERVES 4–6

miso 1 x 200g packet

***kombu* seaweed** 1 stick, chopped into 3 or 4 pieces

boiling water 1.25 litres (2 pints)

buckwheat noodles 100g (3½oz)

TO GARNISH

spring onions small bunch, finely sliced

sesame seeds 2 tbsp, toasted in a hot dry pan for 1 minute

Mung Bean Soup

This simple and light soup was first made for us by an Egyptian friend. It can be made with either fresh or dried mung beans. This is a lovely summer soup served with yogurt or *raita* (*see page* 165).

SERVES 4–6

olive oil 2 tbsp

rosemary 1 sprig, finely chopped

ground coriander 1 tsp

garlic clove 1, crushed

Spanish onion 1 small, finely diced

celery stalk 1, chopped

dried mung beans 200g (7oz), soaked overnight

vegetable stock 1.5 litres (2¾ pints), (*see page* 189)

coriander leaves handful, chopped

lemon juice of 1

1 Infuse the oil with flavour by heating it gently, then adding the rosemary, ground coriander, and garlic, followed quickly by the onion and celery. Sauté for 5–6 minutes.

2 Add the drained mung beans and stock, and simmer for 30 minutes.

3 When the beans are cooked, add the chopped coriander and lemon juice before puréeing with a hand-held blender.

7

Salads

A few people commented that our first book contained very few salad recipes. This reflected the fact that salads represent a relatively small part of The Gate food and menus.

While many of the salads in this chapter make lovely starters by themselves, they often appear on our menus as accompaniments to both main courses and starters, such as the Chickpea and Beetroot Salad (*see page* 135) with Baked Couscous Aubergine (*see page* 75). This demonstrates The Gate philosophy of combining flavours and textures to create a balanced dish.

Salads are not just about leaves and raw vegetables; some of our favourite salads at The Gate are based on cooked vegetables and are served warm. The Warm Root Vegetable Salad (*see page* 143) is a lovely example of cooked vegetables combining beautifully with cold, crisp salad leaves to create one of our most popular winter salads.

Butter Bean, Pickled Lemon, and Mint Salad

The classic "five-bean salad" has given bean salads a rather poor name over the years. At The Gate we regularly use pulses as a base for both salads and salsas. However, it is the fresh herbs and strong seasoning such as the pickled lemon that really bring this dish to life as an accompaniment for grilled vegetables or haloumi cheese.

SERVES 4–6

cooked butter beans 500g (1lb 2oz)

fresh French beans 100g (3½oz), trimmed and blanched

mint small bunch, leaves shredded

DRESSING

olive oil 2 tbsp

pickled lemon 1, diced

banana shallots 2, finely diced

1 For the dressing, combine the olive oil, pickled lemon, and shallot in a bowl and mix well.

2 Toss in the butter beans and French beans and scatter the mint over the top.

Baby Spinach and Roquefort Salad

The Roquefort in this recipe can be substituted by a lighter blue cheese such as dolcelatte or Danish blue.

1 Preheat the oven to 190°C/375°F/gas mark 5.

2 To make the dressing, put the Roquefort, yogurt, lemon juice, and olive oil in a food processor and blend to a smooth, creamy texture.

3 To make the croûtons, trim off the crust, and cut the bread into 1cm (½in) cubes. Drizzle with olive oil and season with salt and pepper. Bake for 10 minutes or until crisp and toasted.

4 Toss the spinach, chives, and avocado together with the cooked croûtons, then drizzle with the dressing.

SERVES 4

ciabatta loaf 1

olive oil 1 tbsp

salt and black pepper

baby spinach 150g (5½oz)

chives 1 bunch, chopped into 1cm (½in) pieces

avocado 1 large, peeled, stoned and cut into 1cm (½in) cubes

DRESSING

Roquefort cheese 55g (2oz)

natural yogurt 2 tbsp

lemon juice 1 tbsp

olive oil 1 tbsp

Globe Artichoke with Honey and Mustard Dressing

For all the fancy work that we have done with artichokes in The Gate's kitchen, there is still something very satisfying about the simplicity of eating a whole globe artichoke leaf by leaf.

1 Boil the artichokes in acidulated water (with the lemon juice or vinegar added) for 15 minutes, or until the hearts are cooked. Drain well.

2 While the artichokes are boiling, make the dressing. Mix all the ingredients together in a bowl until the dressing emulsifies.

3 Serve the artichokes whole on individual plates, and put the dressing in four small dipping bowls alongside.

SERVES 4

globe artichokes 4

lemon juice or white wine vinegar 1 tbsp

DRESSING

Dijon mustard 1 tbsp

olive oil 2 tbsp

runny honey 1 tbsp

lemon juice of 1

garlic clove 1, crushed

Zalata

Zalata literally means "salad" in Arabic. When we were growing up, this classic Middle Eastern salad was the "house salad" served with most meals.

1 Place the chopped red onion in a small bowl with the olive oil, chilli, salt, and pepper.

2 Allow to stand for 15 minutes before adding the tomato, cucumber, lemon juice, and coriander.

SERVES 4–6

red onion 1 small, finely diced

olive oil 2 tbsp

green chilli 1, finely chopped

salt and black pepper

tomatoes 4, cut into 1cm (½in) dice

cucumber 1, cut into 1cm (½in) dice

lemon juice of 1

coriander leaves handful, shredded

Fennel and Peppered Strawberry Salad

This lovely summer salad is a great combination of colours, tastes, and textures. It makes an ideal *hors d'oeuvre* on a summer evening when the British strawberries have come into season.

1 To make the dressing, combine the juices with the olive oil in a bowl.

2 Finely slice the fennel on a mandoline and marinate it in the dressing for 15 minutes.

3 Toss the fennel and its dressing with the watercress and the segmented orange.

4 Dip or roll the strawberries in the black pepper, and use as a garnish around the edges of the salad bowl.

SERVES 4

fennel bulbs 2 medium

watercress 2 bunches

orange 1, peeled and segmented

strawberries 225g (8oz), hulled

cracked black pepper 1 tbsp

DRESSING

lemon juice of 1

orange juice of 1

olive oil 2 tbsp

Warm New Potato Salad

In spring this lovely salad is a real favourite at The Gate, when the new-season potatoes and broad (fava) beans become available.

1 Preheat the oven to 170°C/325°F/gas mark 3. Bake the tomatoes for 20 minutes.

2 While the tomatoes are baking, put the new potatoes in a pan of water, cover, bring to the boil, and cook for about 20 minutes. When cool enough to handle, remove the skins.

3 Meanwhile, pickle the onion crescents by placing them in a bowl with the balsamic vinegar and sugar for 20 minutes.

4 Blanch the shelled beans for 60 seconds in boiling water.

5 When the potatoes and tomatoes are cooked, mix them with all the remaining ingredients in a bowl. Season to taste and serve.

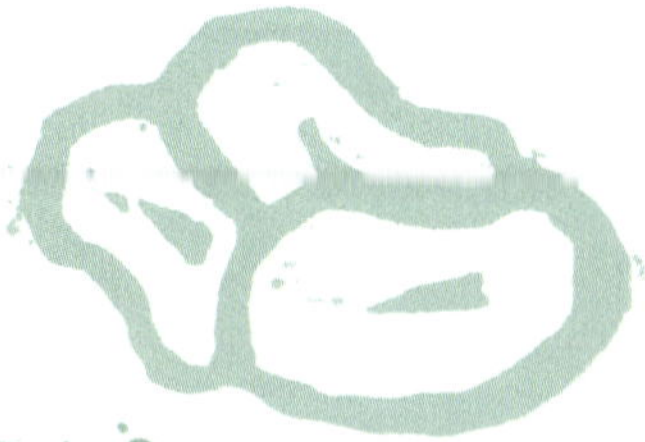

SERVES 4–6

cherry tomatoes 450g (1lb), halved

new potatoes 600g (1lb 5oz)

red onions 2, sliced into thin crescents

balsamic vinegar 3 tbsp

caster sugar 1 tbsp

broad beans 100g (3½oz), freshly shelled

parsley handful, chopped

pitted black olives 100g (3½oz)

olive oil 2 tbsp

Chickpea and Beetroot Salad

Although you can use parboiled beetroot, which is available from most supermarkets, we prefer working with fresh. This salad is inspired by beetroot *kutta* (a traditional Iraqi beetroot and lemon soup). The texture of the chickpeas and the sweetness of the beetroot make it a colourful and tasty salad on its own. At The Gate we often serve it with Baked Couscous Aubergine (*see page* 75).

1 Preheat the oven to 200°C/400°F/gas mark 6.

2 To prepare the beetroot, peel and dice into 1.5cm (⅝in) cubes. Coat with a little of the olive oil and roast for 30 minutes, keeping the tray covered for the first 20 minutes.

3 Allow the beetroot to cool before mixing with the chickpeas.

4 Add the onion, lemon juice, remaining olive oil, the coriander, and mint and mix well.

SERVES 4–6

beetroot 2 medium

olive oil 2–3 tbsp

cooked chickpeas 500g (1lb 2oz)

red onion 1, finely diced

lemons juice of 2

coriander and mint handful of each, finely chopped

Watermelon and Feta Salad

This is an ideal summer dish which reminds us of warm evenings on the *kibbutz,* where a large bowl of this salad would be enjoyed in between drinks and food. It can be served as a starter or as a dessert.

1 Put the feta cubes in a bowl and lightly mix with the olive oil and mint. Leave for 20 minutes or so.

2 To serve, place the chopped watermelon in a large serving platter. Sprinkle with the feta cheese, mint, and olive oil.

SERVES 4–6

feta cheese 500g (1lb 2oz), cut into 1cm (1⁄2in) cubes

olive oil 2 tsp

mint leaves handful, shredded

watermelon 1 small (approx. 2kg / 4 1⁄2lb), peeled and cut into 3cm (1 1⁄4in) cubes

Couscous and Pomegranate Salad

This classic Lebanese salad, which includes one of our favourite fruits, is stunning both visually and on the tastebuds. We often serve this dish with our Middle Eastern platters.

1 Pour the water over the couscous, cover with clingfilm, and leave to soak and absorb the water for 15 minutes.

2 To deseed the pomegranate, cut it into quarters and then release the seeds by pressing against the outside skin. Make sure all the yellow pith is removed because it is very bitter.

3 To make the dressing, combine the olive oil, lemon juice, and salt in a bowl and mix well.

4 Fluff up the couscous using a fork, then pour the dressing over it. Mix in the spring onions, pomegranate seeds, and herbs.

SERVES 4–6

boiling water 250ml (9fl oz)

couscous 150g (5½oz)

pomegranate 1

spring onions 1 bunch, finely sliced

mint and flat-leaf parsley handful of each, shredded

DRESSING

olive oil 2 tbsp

lemons juice of 2

salt 1 tsp

Butter Bean Salad with Tamarind and Yogurt

This moreish sweet-and-sour yogurt dressing is inspired by the cuisine of Kerala in southern India, where this style of dressing is used in many dishes.

1 To make the dressing, mix together the lime juice, tamarind paste, maple syrup, yogurt, and black mustard seeds.

2 Toss together with the butter beans and spring onions.

SERVES 4

butter beans 500g (1lb 2oz), cooked

spring onions 1 bunch, finely chopped

DRESSING

lime juice of 1

tamarind paste 100g (3½oz)

maple syrup 2 tbsp

natural yogurt 250g (9oz), strained

black mustard seeds 1 tbsp, toasted in a hot dry pan for 1 minute

Seared Chicory Salad with Figs and Walnuts

Searing is a lovely technique for removing the bitterness from vegetables such as endive and radicchio. It works as well on the barbecue as it does in the frying pan. The combination of the figs and pecorino (which can be substituted by Parmesan) makes a delightful summer salad.

1 Cut the chicory bulbs in half lengthwise. Mix together half the vinegar and half the oil in a dish and allow the chicory to marinate in this for 15 minutes.

2 Heat a non-stick frying pan. Sear the chicory, cut-side down, for 2–3 minutes, cooking on one side only.

3 Divide the seared chicory and figs among four plates. Sprinkle with the walnuts and pecorino shavings and drizzle the remaining vinegar and oil on top.

SERVES 4

green chicory 4 bulbs

balsamic vinegar 1 tbsp

hazelnut oil 1 tbsp

fresh figs 4, quartered

walnuts 20g (¾oz) shelled, toasted

pecorino cheese 25g (1oz), shaved

Baby Gem Salad with Hazelnuts and Sun-dried Tomatoes

A good salad is all about textures and flavours, and drawing inspiration from the ingredients that you have at hand.

1 Preheat the oven to 200°C/400°F/gas mark 6. To remove the skins from the hazelnuts, roast for 10 minutes or until lightly brown. Place the nuts in a damp tea-towel and rub together until the skins come away from the nuts.

2 To make the dressing, simply combine the ingredients.

3 Toss all the salad ingredients together in a large bowl with the dressing.

SERVES 4

hazelnuts 40g ($1\frac{1}{2}$oz), shelled

baby gem lettuces 6, cores discarded, broken into large pieces

sun-dried tomatoes 35g ($1\frac{1}{4}$oz), thinly sliced

spring onions 1 bunch, finely chopped

feta cheese 100g ($3\frac{1}{2}$oz), cut into cubes

DRESSING

olive oil 2 tbsp

lemon juice of 1

salt pinch

Warm Root Vegetable Salad

In a country such as England it would seem strange to eat only cold salads throughout the year. At The Gate we have developed a number of warm salads, and this is probably the most popular. The combination of the creamy horseradish and the delicate root vegetables works particularly well.

SERVES 4–6

parsnips 2, peeled

swede 1 small, peeled

carrots 2, peeled

olive oil for drizzling

mixed salad leaves 400g (14oz)

pumpkin seeds 75g (2¾oz), toasted in a hot dry pan for 1 minute

DRESSING

fresh horseradish 55g (2oz), grated

crème fraîche 100ml (3½fl oz)

sea salt 1 tsp

1 Preheat the oven to 200°C/400°F/gas mark 6.

2 Cut the vegetables into 3–4cm (1¼–1½in) pieces. Place in a baking tray, drizzle them with olive oil, and bake for about 15 minutes until they just soften. Remove from the oven.

3 To make the dressing, combine the horseradish and crème fraîche in a blender, along with the sea salt.

4 When ready to serve, toss the warm vegetables, salad leaves, and pumpkin seeds together, then pour the dressing over.

Warm Beetroot and Artichoke Salad with Crème Fraîche

This is another of our favourite warm salads, and it is very quick to prepare. The lovely combination of textures, flavours, and electric colours makes this dish a very elegant starter.

SERVES 4–6

Jerusalem artichokes 500g (1lb 2oz)

lemon juice of ½

beetroot 1 large

butter 35g (1¼oz)

salt

white wine splash

crème fraîche 50ml (2fl oz)

TO SERVE

watercress 100g (3½oz)

orange 1, peeled and segmented

1 Peel the artichokes then boil in water to cover, acidulated with the lemon juice, for 15 minutes. Drain and cut the artichokes into 1cm (½in) slices. Peel the beetroot, then slice as thinly as possible (preferably on a mandoline).

2 Fry the artichokes and beetroot together in the butter for 4–5 minutes. Add some salt and a splash of white wine, then allow to reduce by half.

3 Add the crème fraîche to the pan and cook gently until the crème fraîche is nicely melted and you have a beautiful, fluorescent-pink sauce.

4 Serve on a bed of watercress garnished with the segmented orange.

Roasted Butternut Squash and Rocket Salad

The sweetness of the butternut squash with its velvety texture, the pungency of the pumpkin seeds, the nutty oil, and the sweetened shallots with the pecorino make this a lovely yet simple salad combination.

1 Preheat the oven to 200°C/400°F/gas mark 6.

2 Toss the cubed butternut squash in the olive oil, season to taste, and roast for 15 minutes or until slightly tender.

3 Meanwhile, for the dressing, marinate the diced shallots in the balsamic vinegar for 10–15 minutes.

4 Once the butternut squash has cooled, toss it with the rocket, cherry tomatoes, pumpkin seeds, and pecorino shavings. Add the pumpkin-seed oil to the marinated shallots. Drizzle the dressing over the salad and serve.

SERVES 4

butternut squash 500g (1lb 2oz), cut into 2cm (¾in) cubes

olive oil 1 tbsp

salt and black pepper

rocket leaves 400g (14oz)

cherry tomatoes, 1 punnet (about 250g/9oz), halved

pumpkin seeds 75g (2¾oz), toasted in a hot dry pan

pecorino cheese shavings 50g (1¾oz)

DRESSING

shallots 50g (1¾oz), finely diced

balsamic vinegar 1 tbsp

pumpkin-seed oil 2 tbsps

Asian Noodle Salad

This vibrant, quick-to-prepare Asian salad is an excellent accompaniment to whatever you may have on the grill for a summer barbecue, and it also makes a great light lunch in itself.

SERVES 4

egg noodles 500g (1lb 2oz), cooked and refreshed in cold water

carrot 1, cut into julienne strips

mange-tout 100g (3½oz), cut into julienne strips

red pepper 1, deseeded and cut into julienne strips

spring onions 5, cut into julienne strips

beansprouts 55g (2oz)

coriander and mint, handful of each

DRESSING

soya sauce 2 tbsp

caster sugar 1 tbsp

lime juice of 1

red chilli 1, chopped

fresh root ginger 2cm (¾in) chunk, chopped

balsamic vinegar 1 tbsp

sesame oil 2 tbsp

1 To make the dressing, combine all the ingredients in a food processor.

2 Toss the cooked noodles with all the remaining salad ingredients.

3 Mix in the dressing just before serving.

Seaweed Salad and Miso Dressing

There is nothing quite as refreshing as a raw vegetable salad on a hot summer's day. We particularly love this sauce because it works as well in a stir-fry as it does in this salad.

1 For the dressing, using a whisk, combine the *miso* with the soya sauce, maple syrup, and lime juice.

2 Toss the dressing with the carrot, *mooli,* drained seaweed, beansprouts, and coriander. Sprinkle the sesame seeds on top.

SERVES 4

carrot 1 large, cut into julienne strips

mooli 100g (3 ½oz), cut into julienne strips

***wakame* seaweed** 55g (2oz), rehydrated in boiling water

beansprouts 55g (2oz)

coriander handful

black (or white) sesame seeds 1 tbsp

DRESSING

miso 2 tbsp

soya sauce 1 tbsp

maple syrup 2 tbsp

limes juice of 2

Thai Salad

This lovely, vibrant salad was created by our chef, Joe. It is quick to prepare and wonderfully refreshing, and very popular on our summer menu.

SERVES 4–6

mange-tout 100g (3½oz), cut into julienne strips

baby corn 100g (3½oz), cut into quarters lengthwise

beansprouts 100g (3½oz)

green mango 1, peeled, stoned, and cut into julienne strips

pak-choi 4 heads, shredded

mint large handful of leaves, coarsely chopped

coriander small bunch of leaves, coarsely chopped

DRESSING

lemon grass 1 stalk, tough outer leaves removed

fresh root ginger 2cm (¾in) piece

garlic cloves 2

red chillies 2

limes juice of 4

caster sugar 55g (2oz)

soya sauce 75ml (2½fl oz)

1 Place all the prepared salad ingredients into a bowl and toss together well.

2 To make the dressing, place the lemon grass, ginger, garlic, and chillies in a food processor. Blend well, ensuring all the ingredients are finely chopped, before adding the lime juice, sugar, and soya sauce.

3 Pour this dressing over the vegetables and serve.

8

Sauces and Dips

The recipes in this chapter are closest to our hearts and stomachs, and at home on a Friday night we would look in the fridge with excitement to see what chutney or relish had been prepared to go with the evening meal.

So it was natural that we would have a sauce or relish to accompany the dishes that we cooked at The Gate, and in our opinion it is these sauces and salsas that really bring a dish to life.

Classic Pomodoro Sauce

Considering this is probably one of the most cooked sauces in the world, we are still surprised by the number of people who ask for a recipe.

1 Sauté the onion in the oil until translucent: about 6–7 minutes. Add the garlic, carrot, and celery and continue cooking until the carrots and celery are soft: another 5 minutes or so.

2 Add the canned tomatoes, bay leaves, red wine, sun-dried tomatoes, and sugar and gently simmer for 25 minutes.

3 Remove the bay leaves. Add the torn basil and blend to a purée with a hand-held blender.

SERVES 4

Spanish onion 1 large, finely chopped

olive oil 2 tbsp

garlic cloves 2, crushed

carrot 1, finely chopped

celery stalk 1, finely chopped

plum tomatoes 2 x 500g cans

bay leaves 2

red wine splash

sun-dried tomatoes 5

caster sugar 1 tsp

basil handful leaves, torn

Basil and Green Chilli Pesto

This simple variation on the classic pesto Genovese was inspired by the need for a little chilli in every dish. The pesto works beautifully on spaghetti and makes a great addition to sandwiches, and a teaspoon will enliven any sauce. It keeps well in the fridge.

1 Place the basil, chilli, garlic, and 75ml (2½fl oz) olive oil in a food processor and blend until you have a smooth paste.

2 Add the almonds and lemon juice and continue to blend until the almonds are well crushed and integrated.

3 Add the remaining olive oil and season with salt.

SERVES 4

basil 1 large bunch

green chillies 2

garlic clove 1

olive oil 175ml (6fl oz)

shelled almonds 50g (1¾oz), skinned and lightly toasted in a hot dry pan for 1 minute

lemon juice of 1

salt

Mushroom Pâté

This is a lovely, simple, and quick-to-prepare pâté. It is surprisingly rich and satisfying, and makes a delicious *hors d'oeuvre* eaten with a loaf of crusty bread or *crudités* and a glass of red wine.

1 In a pan, melt the butter, then add the garlic and rosemary, quickly followed by the onion. Sauté for 3–4 minutes until the onion is translucent.

2 Add the mushrooms, and once they have begun to emit their liquid, add the white wine and continue to cook until all the liquid has reduced and the mushrooms are nicely glazed.

3 Place the mushrooms in a food processor with the ricotta and dolcelatte, and blend until well combined. Season with salt and pepper.

4 Divide the pâté evenly among four ramekins, smoothing the top with a hot knife. Sprinkle the chopped parsley on top and chill for 2 hours before serving.

SERVES 4

butter 55g (2oz)

garlic clove 1, crushed

chopped rosemary 1 tsp

Spanish onion 1 large, finely diced

Portobello mushrooms 450g (1lb), roughly chopped

white wine splash

ricotta cheese 250g (9oz)

dolcelatte cheese 40g (1½oz)

salt and black pepper

parsley handful, finely chopped

Beetroot and Olive Tapenade

At The Gate we take great pleasure in re-educating our customers' perceptions of certain vegetables. Beetroot certainly comes into this category. It works particularly well in this dish, lending its natural sweetness and bold colour, which give the tapenade a distinctive flavour and appearance.

1 Preheat the oven to 200°C/400°F/gas mark 6. Put the beetroot cubes and olives in a baking tray and bake for 30 minutes.

2 Purée in a blender, adding the olive oil, garlic, and lemon juice. Leave to cool.

SERVES 4

beetroot 1 medium, cut into 2cm (¾in) cubes

pitted black olives 400g (14oz), washed and well drained

olive oil 2 tbsp

garlic clove 1, roughly chopped

lemon juice of 1

Turkish Salad

Turkish salad to us is not Turkish and it is not a salad – it's really more of a relish, usually found on *falafel* stands around Israel. It is sweet, a little spicy, and very piquant. It makes a good complement to *crudités* and fritters, or can be served with *tortillas* or a slice of grilled haloumi.

SERVES 4

red peppers 5

green peppers 2

red chilli 1, finely chopped

red onion 1 large, chopped

olive oil 2 tbsp

tomato purée 100g (3½oz)

caster sugar 2 tbsp

red wine vinegar 2 tbsp

coriander leaves handful, chopped

water 3–4 tbsp

1 To roast and skin the red peppers, preheat the oven to 220°C/425°F/gas mark 7. Oil the peppers lightly and roast them for 15 minutes, turning occasionally.

2 While the red peppers are roasting, the green peppers will need to be charred over a gas flame on the hob (using a skewer or long fork), or cooked under the grill as close to the heat as possible. When they are completely blackened, place in a plastic bag to sweat for 20 minutes. Add the red peppers to the bag when they are ready. This process will allow the skins to be removed very easily.

3 Fry the chilli and then the onion in the oil for 5–6 minutes until the onion is translucent, then add the tomato purée, sugar, vinegar, coriander, and water. Continue to cook for a further 5–6 minutes. Remove from the heat.

4 Skin, deseed, and dice the peppers, and add to the above mixture. Chill for 30 minutes before serving.

Sweet Chilli Sauce

This simple, quick-to-prepare dipping sauce, traditionally served with Thai spring rolls, makes a good accompaniment to many kinds of fritters. It keeps in the fridge for months and can also be used as a dressing for salads or added to stir-fries with a few drops of soya sauce.

1 Put all the ingredients in a small pan with 150ml (5fl oz) water, and bring to the boil.

2 Simmer for 6–7 minutes until the sauce reduces and thickens slightly.

SERVES 4

clear honey 2 tbsp

rice vinegar 2 tbsp

red chilli 1, chopped

lime leaf 1

Harissa

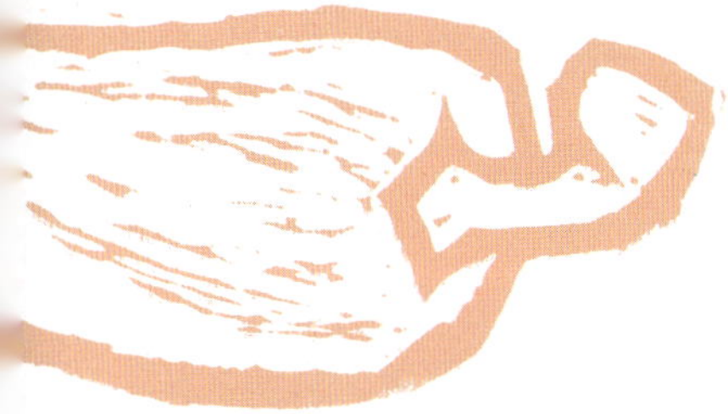

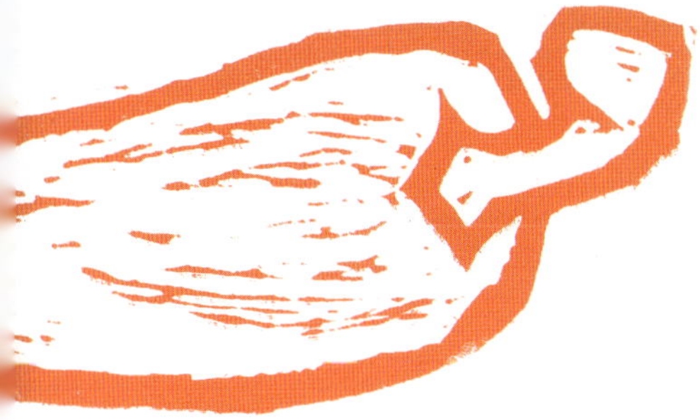

It was not enough to have grown up in a household where chilli was found in most dishes. There was also a chilli sauce with every meal, just in case it wasn't hot enough. A common occurrence at the dinner table was for our mum to bite on a small green chilli and say how hot it was. Then one of our brothers would get her a drink of water, but really all she wanted was another chilli...

1 Preheat the oven to 190°C/375°F/gas mark 5.

2 Place the chilli, red pepper, onion, and garlic in an oven tray and drizzle with the olive oil. Bake for 20 minutes.

3 Allow to cool. Place in a blender and purée, adding the vinegar, coriander, and salt. Serve.

SERVES 4

red chillies 5, sliced

red peppers 2, deseeded and sliced

red onion 1 small, coarsely chopped

garlic clove 1

olive oil 4 tbsp

cider vinegar 1 tbsp

ground coriander 1 tbsp

salt 1 tsp

Lemon Grass Salsa

We came up with this idea somewhat out of adversity to enliven a rather dull soup. It turned out to be something of a eureka moment. This flavour-packed salsa is simple and quick to prepare, and complements a variety of dishes. It also makes an excellent accompaniment to dishes such as grilled vegetables, soups, and *wasabi* potato cakes (*see page* 50).

1 Fry the garlic on its own in a little of the sesame oil until golden brown and slightly crisp. Place in a bowl.

2 Heat the remaining sesame oil and add the lemon grass, chilli, and ginger. Fry for 1–2 minutes, taking care not to burn them. Add the shallot to this and cook for a further 2–3 minutes.

3 Remove the pan from the heat, and stir in the fried garlic, coriander, lime juice, and soya sauce. Leave to cool.

SERVES 4

garlic cloves 2, thinly sliced

sesame oil 3 tbsp

lemon grass stalks 4, outer layers removed, thinly sliced

red chilli 1 large, halved and cut into crescents

fresh root ginger 2cm (¾in) chunk, cut into julienne strips

banana shallots 75g (2¾oz), halved and cut into thin crescents

coriander leaves handful

lime juice of 1

soya sauce 1 tbsp

Tzatziki

We have always been great fans of this tangy yogurt dip. This particular recipe always reminds Adrian of his first girlfriend, who came from a Persian family. Whenever he visited her home there was always a large bowl of *tzatziki* in the fridge, which they would devour with heaps of warm pitta bread.

1 Blend all the ingredients together in a food processor.

2 Allow to stand for half an hour before serving.

SERVES 4

Greek yogurt 350g (12oz), strained

cucumber 1, peeled and seeded

garlic clove 1, crushed

mint leaves handful, finely chopped

lemon juice of 1

salt 1 tsp

Raita

Spending time in India has really developed our appreciation for this simple yogurt dip. It works as a perfect foil for spicy dishes and is just as enjoyable eaten as a dip with pitta bread or spooned into a warm soup.

1 Toast the mustard seeds for 1 minute in a dry frying pan.

2 Place all the ingredients in a bowl, and mix well. Chill for 30 minutes before serving.

SERVES 4

black mustard seeds 1 tsp

natural yogurt 400g (14oz)

mint 2 sprigs, finely chopped

ground coriander 1 tsp

cucumber 1, peeled, deseeded and grated

pickled lemon 1, chopped

salt pinch

Corn Salsa

Corn is one of those vegetables which, while not undereaten, is underutilized, and tends to be cooked in only one way. One of our favourite uses of this vegetable is as a base for salsas, in which the natural sweetness combines very well with the chilli and lime.

1 Brush the sweetcorn with a little of the olive oil and sear in a dry, hot pan until lightly charred in parts. Remove the corn from the cob with a sharp knife. Put into a dish.

2 Heat 1 tbsp of the olive oil in a pan, and lightly sauté the white onion and yellow pepper for 3–5 minutes until slightly softened. Add to the corn.

3 Cook the courgette cubes separately in the remaining oil for 3–4 minutes, and add to the corn.

4 Finally, add the spring onion and lime juice, mix well and serve warm or at room temperature.

SERVES 4

sweetcorn 1 ear

olive oil 2 tbsp

white onion 1 small, finely chopped

yellow pepper 1, deseeded and finely diced

spring onions 4, finely chopped

yellow courgette 1, finely cut into 5mm (¼in) cubes

lime juice of 1

Chipotle Chilli Salsa

There is nothing quite like munching your way through a bowl of tortilla chips with a fresh, homemade salsa and a nice glass of red wine. The *chipotles* – which are large, dried, and smoked jalapeño chillies – can be replaced with regular fresh red chillies, but it is worth going out of your way to find them because their smoky flavour gives the salsa a distinctive finish.

1 Cover the *chipotle* chillies with boiling water and leave to soak for about an hour. Drain well.

2 Place all the ingredients in a food processor and pulse until you have a chunky consistency.

SERVES 4

***chipotle* chillies** 2 dried

plum tomatoes 6, blanched and skinned

red onion 1, finely diced

limes juice of 2

coriander leaves small handful

olive oil 1 tbsp

Apple and Coriander Chutney

Another classic from the family book of chilli sauces. We often prepare this chutney around Passover time, when our utensils and other ingredients are out of commission. With its natural sweetness, it takes minutes to prepare and transforms almost every dish.

1 Blend all the ingredients in a blender, adding a little cold water to help the process if required.

SERVES 4

coriander 1 bunch

green chilli 1

mint handful of leaves

Granny Smith apple 1, peeled, cored, and roughly chopped

garlic clove 1, roughly chopped

lemons juice of 2

salt and black pepper

Mango Amba Chutney

Summer holidays in Israel when we were young were wonderful, but nothing could compare with the excitement and bustle of the old bus station, with its multitude of Middle Eastern fast-food stands. This was a place of great eating, where we would eat *falafel,* among other dishes, but the best part was that you could always help yourself to as much and as many of the pickles and chilli sauces as your palate would allow.

1 Blend the fenugreek powder, 300ml (10fl oz) water, the pickled lemon, garlic, and turmeric to a smooth paste.

2 Add the mango and lemon juice to the blended paste and pulse two or three times. Store in a cool place for 48 hours before serving.

SERVES 4

fenugreek powder 1 tbsp

pickled lemon 1

garlic clove 1

turmeric 1 tsp

green mango 1, peeled, stoned and grated

lemon juice of 1

Mint and Coriander Chutney

Where we grew up, most meals would be served with some kind of chilli sauce on the table. This is one of our favourites. In spite of our chilli obsession, even we realized that not every chutney had to have chilli in it, although the pungent garlic and ginger in this recipe provide a mild background kick.

1 Blend all the ingredients in a blender, adding a little cold water to help the process if required.

SERVES 4

coriander 1 bunch

mint handful of leaves

garlic 1 clove

fresh root ginger 1 tsp, grated

lemons juice of 2

salt and black pepper

Puddings

Traditionally in our family, most meals would end with fresh fruit served as dessert. Each season brought its treats: scented Alphonso mangoes in the spring; melons, peaches, figs, and berries in the summer; and lychees in the autumn. Cooked desserts were reserved for special occasions, when a big tray of *baklava* would be served after the meal with Turkish coffee. It is therefore no coincidence that most of the recipes in this chapter feature fresh fruit.

At The Gate we always serve our desserts with an accompaniment: thick double cream, crème fraîche, a scoop of ice cream, or the perennial favourite crème Anglaise.

White Chocolate Cheesecake

When we were growing up, baked cheesecake was a speciality of the local kosher bakers, most of whom came from Eastern Europe. One could always tell a good cheesecake if it stuck to the roof of the mouth. This cheesecake is much lighter, however – and, being non-baked, it takes almost no time to prepare.

SERVES UP TO 10

white chocolate 500g (1lb 2oz), broken into pieces

Philadelphia cream cheese 600g (1lb 5oz)

double cream 500ml (18fl oz)

caster sugar 100g (3½oz)

BASE

digestive biscuits 15, crushed

butter 85g (3oz), melted

ground cinnamon pinch

1 To make the base, mix together the biscuits, melted butter, and cinnamon. Place in a 25cm (10in) cake tin and press down firmly and evenly across the base of the tin. Chill for 15 minutes.

2 Melt the chocolate in a bowl over a pan of boiling water (the water must not touch the bowl).

3 While the chocolate is melting, put the cream cheese, cream, and sugar in a food processor and blend until you have a smooth, thick texture. Place this in a large mixing bowl, and slowly fold in the soft chocolate until all the ingredients are well combined.

4 Pour into the baking tin on top of the biscuit base. Chill for 3–4 hours before serving.

Pressed Chocolate and Lavender Torte

In recent years we have developed a fascination for using lavender in our desserts. This is a lovely chocolate cake with or without the lavender – and offers the pleasure of taking "produce" from your garden into your kitchen.

1 Melt the chocolate and butter in a bowl over a pan of boiling water (the water must not touch the bowl). Once melted, set aside to cool.

2 Preheat the oven to 180°C/350°F/gas mark 4, and line a 23–25cm (9–10in) cake tin with greaseproof paper.

3 In a separate bowl, place the egg yolks and sugar. Place the bowl over the boiling water and, using the whisk, beat the yolks and sugar together until all the sugar has melted and you have a light-coloured mixture.

4 Beat the egg whites in yet another bowl to the soft-peak stage.

5 First fold the chocolate and lavender into the egg yolks, and then fold this mixture into the egg whites. Pour into the lined cake tin and bake for 45 minutes.

6 With the torte still in the tin, place a small, flat plate over the torte, leaving 1–2cm (½–¾in) around the edge uncovered. Put a heavy object on top to compress the cake until it has cooled and is ready to serve.

SERVES 4

dark chocolate 275g (9¾oz), broken into pieces

butter 175g (6oz)

eggs 8 medium, separated

caster sugar 175g (6oz)

dried lavender 1 tbsp flowers

Apple Charlotte

We have to admit that we are great fans of British puddings, and there is something quite satisfying about turning slices of bread and a few apples from your garden into a great dessert.

1 Preheat the oven to 200°C/400°F/gas mark 6.

2 In a pan, cook the apple, 150g (5½oz) of the sugar, and the cinnamon on a gentle heat for 10–12 minutes until the apples have cooked but not disintegrated.

3 While the apples are cooling, grease four 10cm (4in) ramekins with butter and sprinkle 1 tsp caster sugar over the butter in each.

4 Remove the crust from the bread and cut out eight rounds of bread the same diameter as the ramekins. Cut the rest of the bread into strips 4cm (1½in) wide.

5 Now line each ramekin with a bread round in the base and with strips around the sides, pressing with your fingers to mould the joins together.

6 Place the cooked apple in the bread-lined ramekins, and cover with the final rounds of bread.

7 Bake for 15 minutes. Turn out onto serving plates, and serve hot.

SERVES 4

Bramley apples 500g (1lb 2oz), peeled, cored, and cut into 2cm (¾in) cubes

caster sugar 165g (5¾oz)

ground cinnamon pinch

butter 55g (2oz)

white bread 6 slices

Apple and Blackberry Strudel

This is a recipe that Adrian learned from George Chay, a.k.a. the Strudel King, a distinguished Hungarian gentleman whom he met in his early years of cooking. Once you have mastered this technique, there are an infinite number of different strudels at your disposal. A useful tip is to prepare your strudel on a large sheet of greaseproof paper, using the paper to roll the strudel so as not to puncture it in the process.

SERVES 4

filo pastry 8 sheets

butter 100g (3½oz), melted

icing sugar, for dusting

FILLING

Granny Smith apples 800g (1¾lb)

blackberries 225g (8oz)

caster sugar 150g (5½oz)

lemon zest of 1, finely grated

ground cinnamon pinch

1 Preheat the oven to 180°C/350°F/gas mark 4.

2 Peel, halve, and core the apples for the filling, and slice on a mandoline to 2mm (1/16in) thickness. In a bowl, mix together the sliced apple, blackberries, sugar, lemon zest, and cinnamon.

3 On a clean, flat surface, lay a sheet of filo pastry lengthways, and brush the top side with melted butter. Lay a second filo sheet on top and brush again with butter. Do this again, using the remaining filo, to make three more doubled and buttered filo sheets.

4 Lay the filling at the base of each of the four filo sheets, finishing 5cm (2in) from each edge. Fold in the two ends and roll the pastry over the filling away from you until you have four short rolls.

5 Brush the outside of the pastries with the remaining melted butter, place on a baking sheet, and bake for 15–18 minutes.

6 Dust with icing sugar before serving hot.

Pear, Nectarine, and Raspberry Crumble

Crumbles are for us the quintessential English dessert. At The Gate, we usually poach the hard fruit first so that the crumble can be baked quickly in a few minutes, which prevents the crumble topping from becoming thick and stodgy.

1 Preheat the oven to 220°C/425°F/gas mark 7. Have ready a 23 x 30cm (9 x 12in) baking tray.

2 Put the sugar and 200ml (7fl oz) water into a medium-sized saucepan and bring to the boil. Poach the pear cubes in this syrup for 5–6 minutes or until tender.

3 To make the crumble, place the butter, sugar, and flour in a food processor and blend until you have a sandy texture. Add the almonds and oats.

4 Once the pear has cooled, mix together with the nectarine and raspberries. Place the fruit in the baking tray, and cover with the crumble mix.

5 Bake for 10–12 minutes until the raspberries visibly bubble through the crumble. Serve hot.

SERVES 4

caster sugar 50g (1¾oz)

pears 3, peeled, cored, and cut into 1cm (½in) cubes

nectarines 2, stoned, and cut into large chunks

raspberries 450g (1lb)

CRUMBLE

butter 100g (3½oz), cold and cubed

caster sugar 50g (1¾oz)

plain flour 100g (3½oz)

flaked almonds 55g (2oz)

rolled oats 55g (2oz)

Tarte Tatin

This is a quick recipe and a very enjoyable one to make. Once you have caramelized the fruit and assembled the tart, it can be kept in the fridge ready to be baked at the time of your choice. You can substitute the quinces with apples or pears.

1 Put the quince halves, caster sugar, and water in a pan and poach for 15–20 minutes or until the quince is soft.

2 Preheat the oven to 180°C/350°F/gas mark 4.

3 Spread the butter over the base of a medium tarte tatin tin (flameproof and ovenproof). Sprinkle the muscovado sugar evenly over the butter, then place the quinces flat-side down over the sugar.

4 Place the pan on a low to medium heat, and melt and caramelize the quinces and butter together – this may get a little smoky – about 7–10 minutes.

5 Roll out the pastry, cut a circle the same diameter as the pan, and place over the fruit. Tuck inside the pan, then brush with the egg wash.

6 Transfer the pan to the oven, and bake for 15–20 minutes until the pastry is cooked.

7 Remove the tart from the oven. Place a plate over the top of the pan, and flip the pan over, holding both plate and pan together. Turn the tart over onto the plate. Serve hot.

SERVES 4

quinces 3, peeled, halved, and cored

caster sugar 55g (2oz)

water 75ml (2½fl oz)

butter 100g (3½oz)

dark muscovado sugar 100g (3½oz)

puff pastry 400g (14oz)

egg 1 medium, beaten

Rice Pudding with Roasted Plums

This is another very English dessert that we have come to love, especially in early autumn, when the best plums become available. The comforting combination of the soft, creamy rice and caramelized fruit is a perfect end to a meal.

1 Preheat the oven to 170°C/325°F/gas mark 3.

2 To roast the plums, cut each in half, stone them, then place in a small baking tray. Sprinkle each with ½ tsp sugar and roast for 15–20 minutes.

3 Meanwhile, to make the rice pudding, in a pan bring the milk and cream to the boil with the vanilla and cardamom. Add the rice and cook gently for 15 minutes, stirring occasionally. Finally, add the caster sugar.

4 To serve, fill a 7.5cm (3in) ramekin with the rice pudding and turn over onto a large plate. Do the same on three other plates. Place the plum halves around and drizzle with the plum syrup.

SERVES 4

milk 250ml (9fl oz)

double cream 250ml (9fl oz)

vanilla extract 1 tsp

cardamom pods 2, crushed

pudding rice 100g (3½oz)

caster sugar 90g (3¼oz)

ROASTED PLUMS

Victoria or other large plums 8

caster sugar 4 tsp

Hazelnut and Stem Ginger Biscotti

We think of biscotti as doggie treats for humans! Once made, they will keep in a sealed jar for over a month, and make a lovely accompaniment to simple desserts such as *brûlée* or mousse, and of course go beautifully with the morning espresso...

1 Preheat the oven to 200°C/400°F/gas mark 6.

2 In a food processor, mix together the flour, sugar, eggs, and baking powder. Once the ingredients have been well mixed, place in a bowl and stir in the nuts, ginger, and lemon zest.

3 Mould the mixture into a log 3cm (1¼in) wide, wrap, and chill in the fridge for 30 minutes.

4 Bake the log for 30 minutes. Remove from the oven, and reduce the oven temperature to 180°C/350°F/gas mark 4.

5 Cut the log into thin slices, about 3mm (⅛in) thick. Place these slices on a baking tray, return to the oven, and bake for a further 15 minutes. Cool on a wire rack.

MAKES ABOUT 25–30 BISCUITS

plain flour 300g (10½oz), sifted

caster sugar 200g (7oz)

eggs 3 medium

baking powder 1 tsp

shelled hazelnuts 150g (5½oz), roasted and skinned (*see page* 142)

stem ginger in syrup 150g (5½oz), drained, and thinly sliced

lemon zest of 1, finely grated

STORE CUPBOARD

You will probably have many of the following already in your store cupboard, but this is a sort of *aide-memoire* to the ingredients that we use in our cooking.

Oils, vinegars, and other liquid flavourings

Balsamic vinegar
This sweet Italian vinegar, made from red wine and traditionally from the city of Modena, is lovely and less acidic than most. It is often used in marinades and salad dressings.

White wine vinegar
Lighter in colour than balsamic and lighter in flavour than both balsamic and cider vinegars, we use this in dressings and marinades.

Cider vinegar
This basic vinegar made from apples is used mainly in our kitchen for acidulating vegetables when cooking.

Rice vinegar
A more robust vinegar than the others, this is also slightly less acidic. We use it in dressings mainly.

Mirin
A sweet rice wine from Japan, *mirin* is an important constituent when making *sushi,* and is a subtle and valuable addition to marinades and dressings.

White wine
An important ingredient. If you are like Adrian and generally drink red wine, you don't want to open a whole bottle. A clever idea is to freeze any leftover white wine in ice cubes, ensuring you have it available when required, usually for sauces. Needless to say, the nicer the wine, the nicer the sauce...

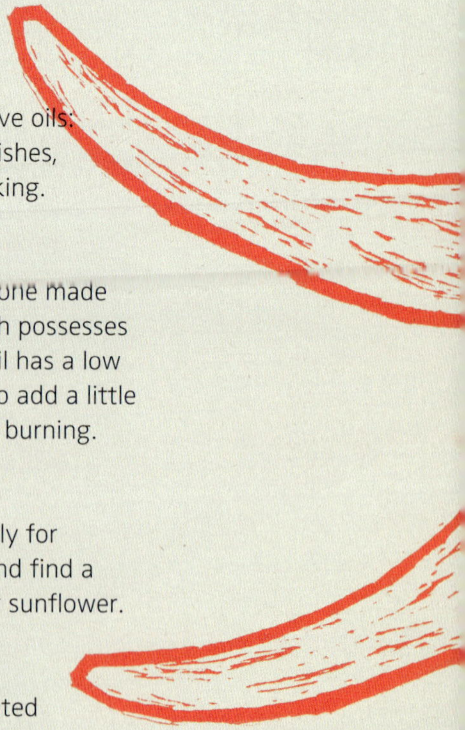

Olive oil
Generally we use two types of olive oils: extra-virgin for salads and cold dishes, and a cheaper non-virgin for cooking.

Sesame oil
Always use a pure oil, preferably one made from toasted sesame seeds, which possesses a unique nutty flavour. Sesame oil has a low burning point, and a good tip is to add a little olive oil when cooking to prevent burning.

Vegetable oil
Generally we use vegetable oil only for deep-frying. Avoid blended oils and find a pure vegetable oil such as corn or sunflower.

Soya sauce
One of a number of products created from fermented soya beans. It is worth finding a good sauce, and at The Gate we use Kikkoman.

Herbs and spices

Herbs and spices, fresh and dried, home-grown and bought, are essential in The Gate style of cooking.

Basil, thyme, rosemary, tarragon, and chives

These herbs originate mostly from the Mediterranean side of Europe. They bring freshness and vitality to dishes, and are constantly used in our cooking. Strictly speaking, most of them should be fresh, picked from the garden or window box, and stored in the fridge if necessary.

Coriander

These pungent, fresh green leaves are essential for Middle Eastern and Asian cooking.

Chillies

Chillies – fresh or dried – are constantly used in our cooking. Bear in mind that small chillies tend to be much hotter that the larger ones. You can deseed them first if you don't like it *too* hot, and in all the recipes we have left this up to you to decide. *Chipotle* chillies and plain dried chilli flakes are useful store-cupboard ingredients, used in salsas and sauces. When fresh, green chillies are slightly sharper in flavour than red (they are less mature), and red are a little sweeter.

Galangal, lime leaves, and lemon grass

Galangal is a Thai herb that looks very similar to ginger, but has a slight aniseed flavour. Lemon grass and lime leaves are also frequently used in our food, and bring their own unique tastes and aromas. Although Thai herbs can be a little difficult to find, they do store well in the freezer.

Garlic and ginger

These provide the cornerstone of Eastern and Western cooking. Fresh root ginger is used in curries and sauces, but we also use stem ginger, which is fresh root that has been sugar-preserved. Delicious, too, is the Japanese pink pickled ginger.

Dried flowers

We use dried flowers such as lavender and rose petals sparingly and occasionally, and they are easily procured from your (or your neighbour's) garden.

Dried spices

These are constantly used in our cooking. Dried spices such as caraway, cumin, coriander, cardamom, cinnamon, turmeric, fenugreek, star anise, and mustard and *ajowan* seeds are usually best bought whole, then freshly roasted, and milled to bring out their true flavours. Mixtures of dried spices such as garam masala can be bought, but are best made freshly. Many spices come only in ground form, such as paprika (best when smoked).

Horseradish

Wasabi, the Japanese horseradish, comes as a light-green powder and simply rehydrates with water. It also comes as a paste in a tube. Our Western horseradish comes from a root, which can be bought fresh (peel and grate very carefully: it is very hot and will make you cry), or already grated in jars.

Tamarind

This is a sour fruit that grows in most places in Asia, and is used extensively in cooking. It can be found as a paste or in a dried block, and both are available in most Asian grocery stores. To use the dried block, dissolve a measured piece in hot water, and then sieve.

Vanilla pod and vanilla extract

Vanilla pods are consummately luxurious, even just to smell, but they are hard to find, and expensive. A good extract (*not* essence) is a good substitute.

Other Important Ingredients

Butter

We generally use unsalted for desserts.

Eggs

These are generally medium, and we buy free-range and organic.

Seaweeds

Kombu and *wakame* are freely available now, not just in Japanese stores. These dried seaweeds don't have the same salty flavour as fresh, but they are still tasty, and very nutritious.

Nuts and seeds

Pistachio, cashews, almonds, pine nuts, walnuts, and sesame seeds (black and white) provide an important source of protein in a vegetarian diet, but in our kitchen they are also important ingredients in the cooking of savouries and sweets. Try to buy them in the shell, because they will be fresher. Dry-toasting before use brings out an inherent nuttiness in most nuts and seeds.

Sugars and sweeteners

Caster sugar is used mainly for desserts, and muscovado sugar – both light and dark – we use in marinades and other dishes where we want a deeper flavour. Honey, usually clear, and maple syrup are used for dressings.

Rices and grains

Rice is our carbohydrate of choice. We use arborio for risotto, and basmati or jasmine, both with their distinct fragrances, with curries and other spicy dishes.

Of the other grains that we use, couscous is a favourite. It is a "processed" wheat that is very quick to prepare, only needing to be soaked in hot water for about 15–20 minutes. Pearl barley is useful, too, but it needs to be cooked for about 40 minutes.

Grains and pulses

We use cannellini beans, chickpeas, butter beans, broad (fava) beans, and mung beans. For spontaneous meals, it is worth having a few cans in the store cupboard, but we are old school and would generally use dried beans that require a minimum of 12 hours' soaking in water before cooking. If using mung beans, you'll *have* to buy them dried (or fresh, if you're lucky), and it's essential to have dried broad beans for the *falafel*. Canned lentils are not good, so buy dried and cook them in 15 minutes.

Flours

We always keep a selection of flours for different uses: a strong white flour for bread, buckwheat flour for blinis and fritters, chickpea flour (or gram, available in Asian groceries) for *pakoras*, and polenta (a maize flour) for making polenta and corn bread. We usually buy the "pronto" polenta for quick cooking. We also use cornflour in cooking and things like tempura batters.

Jars, packets, and cans

Coconut milk
We find this invaluable in our store cupboard. It comes in small 200ml cans, and is best used for curries and spicy dishes.

Dried ceps or porcini
These add enormous flavour to stocks and sauces. They need to be rehydrated for 30 minutes in boiling water. Keep the water because it is full of flavour.

Pickled lemons
These can be found in good delis and Asian grocery stores. The major flavour is in the peel, but you can use the whole thing in stews, salads, and sauces.

Vegetable stock
A good-quality vegetarian stock, Marigold, is available in granule form for soups. Always use less than suggested to avoid its flavour overpowering your soup.

To make a quick, light vegetable stock, chop 1 large leek, 2 sticks of celery, 2 carrots, 1 tomato, and 2 bay leaves into 2cm (¾in) pieces, and put in 1½ litres (1¾ pints) of water. Season with salt and pepper. Bring to the boil, then reduce the heat to a simmer. Put a lid on the pan and simmer for 10–15 minutes, then drain.

Tomatoes
Tomatoes are available in several forms – fresh, canned (plum and chopped), as paste or purée, and sun-dried (also in several forms). We actually like to buy dehydrated dried tomatoes and rehydrate them ourselves: we cook them gently in a little olive oil with some garlic and a few fresh herbs. They are much cheaper, and much less oily, and enhance flavours when added to pasta sauces. Canned tomatoes we usually use in sauces: they are cooked down to a paste. We would generally choose sun-dried tomato paste these days rather than tomato purée, although the latter can be useful.

Pastry
Filo and puff pastry are useful, and it's worth keeping a packet of each in the freezer.

Dried fruit
We use apricots, prunes (usually from Agen), raisins, and sultanas. When buying, go for organic, or buy in health-food stores, because many everyday brands are coated in preservatives and oil, the taste of which can really mar a dish.

INDEX

Glossary entries are shown with **bold** page numbers

Acknowledgments

With special thanks to Diana Daniel, Joe Tyrrell, and Jude Harris

Adrian and Michael Daniel